Regardless of what you were
taught to believe

THERE IS
NOTHING WRONG
WITH YOU

for Ramada
and
for Walter
in gratitude

- printed on recycled paper -

Published by

Keep It Simple Books

P.O. Box 91, Mtn. View, CA 94042

INTRODUCTION

When I began guiding people along a path of spiritual growth, I realized that much of my role was to be an external representative of the unconditional love and acceptance they were seeking to find in themselves. I also realized early on that they didn't know what they were seeking, or that I was playing that role. So we proceeded with the teacher representing the loving, structure-providing, safe mother/father, as well as the wise, compassionate savior who would give them peace, clarity and freedom.

SOME QUICKLY CONCLUDED that I could not give them what they were looking for and moved on to find someone who could. Others stuck it out, and slowly, step by courageous step, grew to see that no one could give them what they were seeking because it was already theirs, already within them. They found that the work was to realize it for themselves. A teacher could only point the way.

Over the years I've come to see that what I'm doing as guide is trying to get folks to turn loose of the conditioning they have received that says they are bad, wrong and inadequate long enough for them to catch a glimpse of who they really are. It's only after years of learning to trust _my_ perceptions that they can begin to accept the possibility that their beliefs about themselves and their world might be less than completely accurate.

Every spiritual path tells us that what we are seeking is inside us. Society, the world, others, conditioning teaches us as children to stop looking to ourselves in order to know what is so for us, and to begin to look to others in order to know what is right. We first learn to look to parents, then teachers, then friends, lovers, husband or wife, children, Jesus or the Buddha or god— all "out there." The love, the acceptance, the approval is out there and must be earned somehow.

Once we have completed the turn away from ourselves, away from our Heart, we experience ourselves as separate and find ourselves in a fight for survival. I am now a small self adrift in a huge, threatening world. All my focus must be on surviving.

Society offers us help in the form of various techniques and processes designed to enable us to cope better. But some of us—I would say the lucky ones—can't learn to cope. We keep having a nagging, unsettling sense that there is something fundamentally wrong with the whole structure. "It's not just that I am wrong.

It feels bigger than that."

This deep down dissatisfaction will sometimes lead a person to consider the realm of the spirit. "Maybe it's even bigger than I thought."

The reason spiritual practice is essential in doing this work of going beyond self-hate is that, in order to be free of self-hate, we must find the unconditional. We may not have the words or the concepts, but what we are longing for is something greater than this world, something lasting and secure. Of course, egocentricity (the illusion that you are separate from everything else) begins by thinking it can find this for itself, but, initially, that doesn't matter. It's the looking that matters, not who is looking or what is being looked for.

Egocentricity is conditional. It is dualistic.

It is the process of believing oneself to be separate. An illusion of separateness is not capable of experiencing wholeness.

A spiritual practice, if we are willing and patient and sincere, will eventually lead us to that which can embrace the egocentric, conditioned belief in separateness.

As we learn to sit down, sit still and pay attention, we begin to glimpse that which sees through the illusion, beyond the voices of society's conditioning, back to the original being. And slowly that perceiving becomes more real than all you've been taught to believe. You begin to cease identifying with the small, frightened, socialized, conditioned person you have always thought was the real you, and you begin to see with a much broader view.

With practice, you will move from being one who is hoping and looking to be saved to that which can save. You will begin to be the love, acceptance and compassion you have always sought.

In loving kindness,
Cheri

ACKNOWLEDGMENTS

All these people have made, and continue to make, so many contributions it is impossible to list them in all the categories in which they participate. For instance, Nancy heads up InnerVision East, trains our facilitators and guides workshops and retreats; Tricia runs the Zen Center, coordinates InnerVision and facilitates Going Beyond Self-Hate groups; Chris designed our building, guides the Asheville, NC, sitting group and facilitates workshops; the monks do it all. You get the idea...

So, deep gratitude to:
Christa - for everything
Nancy Spence - InnerVision partner, Dharma friend and teacher for 20 years
Phil and Cameron - monks whose devotion to a spiritual practice inspires us all
Tricia, Cass, Jan - coordinators and organizers extraordinaire

Tom and Greg - master builders of
    monasteries and retreat centers
Chris and Rich - Zen architect, Zen contractor
Erin and Jennifer - curriculum developers
Ann - among the world's most patient
    computer wizards
Sara - for doing what she does so well
Penny, Tom, John, Aurelia and Payson, Lynn
    and Ellen, Elizabeth, Melinda, Jeannie,
    Susan - for countless gifts
Facilitators: Ann, Jan, Nancy, Jean, Mae,
    Jan, Karen, Margaret, Arthur, Melinda,
    Sandy, Joe, Jan, Darlene, Mary, Jackie,
    Chris, Mary Ellen, Dennis, Betsy, Janet,
    Maggie
Our far-flung Sangha in Calaveras County,
    Mountain View, San Francisco, San Diego,
    Sonora, Burbank, North Carolina

This book follows the same format as all the other books I have written.

That format is: LOOSE ORGANIZATION
                 (kind of like life)

What organization there is goes something like this:

    What self-hate is
    How we learn self-hate
    Forms self-hate takes
    How to go beyond self-hate

This book is offered in loving kindness.

You've been taught
that there is something wrong with you
and that you are imperfect,
but there isn't
and you're not.

Unless you were
raised by wolves,
the chances are extremely good that
as you were growing up you heard at
least a few of the following:

Don't do that... Stop that... Put that down
... I told you not to do that... Why don't you
ever listen... Wipe that look off your face
... I'll give you something to cry about...
Don't touch that... You shouldn't feel that
way... You should have known better...
Will you ever learn... You should be
ashamed of yourself... Shame on you...
I can't believe you did that... Don't ever
let me see you do that again... See, that
serves you right... I told you so... Are
you ever going to get it... What were the
last words out of my mouth... What were
you thinking of... You ruin everything...
You have no sense... You're nuts. The
nurses must have dropped you on your
head... Just once, do something right...

2

I've sacrificed everything for you and what thanks do I get... I had great hopes for you... If I've told you once, I've told you a thousand times... Give you an inch, you take a mile... Anybody would know that..
  Don't talk back to me ... You'll do as you are told... You're not funny... Who do you think you are.... Why did you do it that way ...You were born bad... You drive me crazy ... You do that just to hurt me ... I could skin you alive... What will the neighbors say... You do that to torture me... You're so mean...I could beat the daylights out of you... Don't you dare look at me ... You little brat... You make me hate you... It's all your fault... You make me sick ... You've trying to kill me... Now what's the matter with you, cry baby ... Go to your room... You deserve it... Eat it because children are starving... Don't stick your lip out... If you cry, I'll slap you... Don't you ever think about anyone else.... Get out of my sight... and on and on and on and on and on and on .

3

Somewhere along the line you concluded
that there was something wrong
with you.

OF COURSE YOU DID!

WHAT ELSE COULD YOU CONCLUDE!

If there were nothing wrong
with you,

PEOPLE WOULDN'T TREAT YOU THAT WAY!
THEY WOULDN'T SAY THOSE THINGS TO YOU!

"Then why did they do that to me?"

Because it was done to them.
Because we do
            what we've been taught.

Society calls this
"childrearing"
or
"socialization".

We call it
"sad".

Most people hold
an unshakable belief
that the primary reason
they are "good" is that
they punish themselves
when they are "bad".

Without punishment,
bad would win out
over good.*

*This entire book is based on the premise
that this is not true.

7

Child
is
born.

Child learns to
turn away from
self toward other
to get needs met.
(stops trusting
intuitive knowing)

Child
is
reborn.

Person finds
compassion and
self acceptance

Need is not met;
child believes it is
because s/he is bad.

Child abandons self and
decides to be perfect
(be who others want)
"I just won't need anything."
"I shouldn't be afraid."
"I'll do everything right."

Awareness
work

Person tries
everything to
make conditioning
work.

Child begins to develop
survival behaviors. These
behaviors are self-denying,
self-preserving, self-
destructive. (shuts down
emotionally; eats to stuff
feelings; etc.)

Suffering

Individual uses self-hating
behaviors to try to be a
good person. (values others
over self; denies self
unnecessarily; uses ideals
against self)

Underline What underline happened underline to underline you, not who you are, makes you angry, fearful, greedy, mean, anxious, etc.

We learned behaviors in order to survive. We were taught to hate those behaviors and to see them as signs of our badness. Yet we must keep doing them because they still mean survival to us. And we hate ourselves for doing them.

THE TRAP:
    I believe I must be this way
        to survive.
    I hate myself for being this way.

RESULT:
    self-hate = survival
    survival = self-hate

9

The process of self-hate
is so much a part of the average person
that we don't even recognize it.

We think we're just doing the things
that will insure we'll be good.
It's normal, we say.
Everybody does it.
Or should.

If you want to know
what happened to you,
look at how you treat yourself now...

That was a dumb
thing to do.

Won't I ever
learn?

I shouldn't
feel like this.

I should know
better.

Does that mean
someone consciously, deliberately
did that to you?

Perhaps not.

But you got the message anyway,

didn't you?

It is confusing for someone to
conclude that they aren't loved
because there is something
wrong with them.

"I want to be loved, but
there's something wrong with me.
I need to fix that - even though
I'm not really sure I know what it is
or how to fix it.
But I must keep trying anyway
because I really want to be loved."

This person who is trying to become
lovable spends much
time, attention and energy
trying to
be good, earn approval, please others,
BE PERFECT.

⇨

It's like being on a journey
and being completely lost –
going . . .

In the wrong direction
but making really good time.

It is a blessing
to be confused.

Confusion is the result of attempting
to cling to illusion
in the face of
what you are seeing
to be true for you.

If you will continue to look,
the confusion
will give way to clarity.

And the clarity is compassion.

SOME OF THE FORMS SELF-HATE TAKES

◆ SABOTAGE

You try to do something good for yourself or for someone else and somehow manage to turn the whole thing against yourself. You keep doing the very things you didn't want to do or don't approve of, and you can't seem to figure out how you do that. It's a perfect system for self-hate because:

1) You're operating out of an ideal.
2) You don't live up to your ideal.
3) You can't figure out what you're doing wrong.

◆ TAKING BLAME BUT NOT CREDIT

If something goes well, it's a gift from God. If it goes badly, it's all your fault. And even if you do take a little credit for something, you can always avoid feeling good about it by finding what could have been done better.

◆ BLAMING OTHERS

Self-hating and "other" hating are the same thing. Whether you are hateful toward others or hating yourself directly, it's self-hate— you are always the recipient.

◆ KEEPING SECRETS

You don't let other people know what's going on inside you so that you can be in there beating yourself with it.

♦ HARBORING SECRET WOUNDS
   You review old hurts and injustices rather than being present to yourself now.

♦ NOT BEING ABLE TO RECEIVE
   Gifts, compliments, help, favors, praise, etc. are things you have difficulty allowing yourself to have.

♦ SEEING WHAT IS WRONG WITH EVERYTHING
   Your habit is to find fault, criticize, judge and compare. Remember, what is is all that is. The alternate reality in which everything is exactly as you think it should be exists only in your mind, and it exists primarily to torture you.

♦ TRYING TO BE DIFFERENT
   Just being who you are, your "plain old self," isn't enough. You feel you have to maintain an image.

♦ ATTEMPTING TO BE PERFECT

♦ BEING ACCIDENT PRONE
   Your attention is so often focused on some other time, person or thing that you injure yourself in the present. You don't feel you deserve your attention. Others are more important.

♦ CONTINUING TO PUT YOURSELF IN ABUSIVE SITUATIONS

Even if you realize that you have this pattern, your fear and self-hate are too strong to let you break out of it.

♦ MAINTAINING AN UNCOMFORTABLE PHYSICAL POSITION

You hold your shoulders in a way that creates pain. You clench your teeth. You "sit small" on the bus so as not to intrude into anyone else's space. You continue to sit in an uncomfortable chair at work because you don't want to make waves.

♦ MAINTAINING AN UNCOMFORTABLE MENTAL POSITION

Clinging to "shoulds:" "It's not right to be happy when there is so much suffering in the world." "People should say please and thank you." "Children deserve to have two parents."

≈ ♥ ≈

SOME VOICES AND GESTURES AND ACTIONS OF SELF-HATE

A word or gesture can conjure up a whole lifetime of negativity or defeat or unworthiness. When the memories and emotions tied to that word or gesture arise, it's like having a truckload of self-hate dumped on you.

♦ "I can't believe you did that! What's the matter with you?"

♦ "God, Cheryl!" (tone of disgust)

♦ A shrug of the shoulders and the words "It doesn't matter." (Signals total defeat.)

♦ A sinking feeling of "I've done something wrong," and a feeling of panic, "What's the right thing to do?"

♦ Buying anything for anyone else but never anything for myself.

♦ Wanting to eat something and a voice saying, "Can't you ever say no to yourself?" and realizing that I say no to myself all the time about everything except food.

≈ ♥ ≈

By way of explanation –

In this book we refer often to "the voices inside your head" or similar phrases.

We aren't talking about a psychological disorder.

"Voices inside the head" refers to the nearly endless stream of thoughts that beset us all, the constant flow of judgments, ideas, criticism, opinions that we tell ourselves day in and day out.

AND WE WANT TO EMPHASIZE
that it is important not to believe that these "voices" have helpful information for you about yourself!

Egocentricity uses many voices to draw us into self-hate.

VOICE

Nothing subtle about it
"You're disgusting. You make me sick."

VOICE

Sounds like normal, helpful,
constructive criticism
"It was stupid of me to have said
that. I must watch what I say."
(Children learn early to call themselves and others "stupid".)

VOICE

Self-discipline; helpful in keeping us
on the right track
"I must finish this now even though
I'm exhausted. I must not give in to
these little self-indulgences. Who
knows where it would stop."

VOICE

Really, really true and helpful;
the voice of clarity and wisdom
Example: You read a book that is,
for you, spiritually meaningful.
Every sentence is translated into,
"I should be like that." This voice
might start out sounding sincere
but soon slides into accusation.
"I've been doing it wrong all this
time. What's wrong with me?"
Another example: Sitting in
meditation you might be quiet
and comfortable, just breathing.
Then this voice says, " I don't
think I'm doing this right. If I
were, my attention wouldn't
wander."

⇨

You can listen to the voices
that say there is something
wrong with you,

It's actually very helpful
to be aware of them,

JUST
DON'T
BELIEVE
THEM!

Most of what we have been

TAUGHT TO BELIEVE

we had to be

TAUGHT TO BELIEVE

BECAUSE·IT·ISN'T·TRUE.

This is why children have to be
conditioned so heavily!
WE WOULD NEVER HAVE REACHED
THESE CONCLUSIONS ON OUR OWN!

If we could for a moment
look at what we've been taught to
believe with an unconditioned mind,
we would see that not only is it
not true,
it's absurd.

SO,

what happened?

→

1.

The child has a need.

EXAMPLE:

The child is afraid.
Fear becomes a "subpersonality", a
permanent aspect of this child's
personality; a defense mechanism; a
part of the child's survival system.

20

The need is rejected.

The need does not get met by the person who is looked to to meet it. The child is traumatized when this happens.
The trauma / rejection becomes a subpersonality.

3.

The child comes up with a behavior as a means of survival in order to get the need met.

EXAMPLE:

If the child is afraid of the dark, she/he will get up and sneak a flashlight into the bed.
This behavior becomes a subpersonality.

The child identifies with the authority figure who didn't meet the need and, at the same time, identifies with the part who was rejected.

The belief that is born is:

"There must be something wrong with me. That's why they are treating me this way. It's my fault. It's not their fault; there can't be anything wrong with them because my survival depends on them."

THIS IS THE BIRTH OF SELF-HATE.

5.

The child decides to be perfect, to do everything right, to be really good in order to be loved. There is no choice about this; the child's survival depends on it.

"They don't love me because there is something wrong with me. If I just do it right and never let that happen again, then they'll love me."

THIS SELF-TALK MAINTAINS SELF-HATE.

"The Judge" as a subpersonality is born to make sure that the child is perfect and right and good in order to survive.

The birth of the judge guarantees the continued existence of self-hate.

This process is constantly repeating up through about age 7 when, it is said, we are completely socialized. After that, the judge is tenured and guaranteed a full-time job.

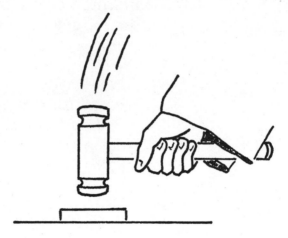

During this process we have concluded that
    needs are bad,
    we are bad for having them.

And, of course, we have them anyway.

STUDENT: Recently you used the term "horrible, needy thing," and I realized that that's exactly how I think of it: needy is horrible. No wonder I can't let neediness come up in myself. And when I see it in others, I slam them down with the same judgment that it's horrible and unacceptable.

HORRIBLE
NEEDY
THING

GUIDE: That's an example of the conclusion we drew when we first began learning to abandon ourselves. We concluded that the reason we were being rejected was that we had a need, and having a need means you're bad. If you're bad, you're unlovable, and if you're unlovable, you won't be able to survive. So from that perspective, the bottom line is: Don't have needs.

≈ ♥ ≈

Once our attention has been turned
outward, most of us never address
the original need we left behind.
In order to get someone else to meet it.

In order to survive, we learn to abandon
the need REPEATEDLY
              and
          COMPLETELY
even though no one else ever meets it!

Most of us don't know that it is that
need that has been controlling our lives.

          The need? TO BE LOVED
                    AND ACCEPTED
                    EXACTLY AS WE ARE.

Eventually it dawns on us that we can't stay in the "I'm wrong" mode forever or we really won't survive. There has to be a duality formed in which "I'm not wrong; they are wrong" operates.

The sadness is that you can live your whole life trying to prove your parents wrong, but nothing will really have changed. All your ideas about being perfect and right and good will just be in reaction to the conditioning you received from your parents. Not only will you pursue their ideas of perfection, but you will have to reject those ideas, and you will have to reject them perfectly, and pretty soon you will have tied yourself up in such a knot that you won't be able to move in any direction, and you will just sit there in self-hate because the bottom line is

"you lose."

STUDENT: Why can't I ever let myself off the hook? Why do I never feel that I have been good enough, generous enough? I try and try but this little nagging guilty feeling is always here.

GUIDE: Good question. I look at this a lot. It's just so pervasive in human experience. I was talking about it earlier and gave this example:

You go along in life and you do what you've supposed to do. And every time you do something you've supposed to do, you put a dollar in the bank. Okay. Every time you're kind, patient, or you do the thing you've supposed to do — whatever it is (you know what those things are for you) — every time, you put a dollar in the bank, a dollar in the bank, a dollar in the bank...

35

And you're working at this! You're up
early in the morning doing these
things until late at night. Every day.

Finally, you feel like you've just kind of
worn out. You feel like you need a
little pleasure in your life, a little
time on the beach or something.
And so you think,
"I'm going to go
to the bank, and
I'm going to take
out some money,

and I'm going to do something nice for
myself."

So you go to the bank and you say,
"Here I am. I want to take out some

of the money I've saved so that I can do something nice for myself."

And the response is, "Oh no. You haven't earned nearly enough to get anything for yourself. Oh, you have to work much harder — you have to put much, much more money in before you can get anything for yourself."

REQUEST DENIED

REASON:
INSUFFICIENT FUNDS

And, of course, if this were First National you were dealing with, you would say, "No, this not the way this is going to work. This is my money. You can't tell me when and

and where and how I can spend it. "
And yet,
    with this system
        of self-hate
            that's _exactly_
                what's going on!
You get to earn and earn and earn
endlessly
            and there is never
            a pay back.
You think that you've saving up all
these points, and that some day
you'll receive some benefit from them,
                but you never do.

STUDENT: Yes. I can see that I do that
to myself, and it seems like I do it
a lot, really a lot.

GUIDE: Let me give you another
example.
                                ⇨

You decide that you're going to take up running...
And so this person is going to help you become a runner.
So you put on your little outfit and the person says:

} Why'd you put that on?
} Boy, do you look stupid in that!
} You're going to wear that?

Well, you go put on another outfit— you put on several outfits and finally just give up on that discussion. You're never going to <u>look</u> good enough to run so you just decide you're going to do it anyway.

You go out there and start running, and the person says:

You call that running?
Whatever made you think you
could be a runner?

Now, I just want to give you an
opposite possibility, okay?

How about
if the person who is with you says:

Run in anything, it doesn't
matter. You look fine. Just
get out there and run. That's
great! You've doing good.
How long did you run? Ten
minutes? That's wonderful!

Think about it!
⇩
Which person wants you to run,
and
which person wants you not to run?

THERE'S NO MYSTERY
IN THIS,
FOLKS!
It's not hard to pick out which
characters are in which camp.
INTERNALLY OR EXTERNALLY!
In the first example, the person at
the bank DOES NOT LIKE YOU!

★ It's important to get that! ★

It's not like this person is really pulling
for you to get enough money in the bank
to do something special for yourself.

NO!
THIS PERSON
IS NEVER GOING
TO GIVE YOU
A DIME!
YOU WILL WORK YOURSELF TO DEATH,
AND YOU'LL NEVER GET A THING FOR IT.
IT IS REALLY IMPORTANT
TO UNDERSTAND THAT!

If you had a person
  in your life

treating you the way
      you treat yourself,

      you would have gotten
      rid of them

      a long

      time

      ago...

STUDENT: You'd think so, wouldn't you?

GUIDE: It seems so clear, but because that voice speaks from inside our own heads, we are actually willing to perpetuate the illusion that this person:
- is on our side
- likes us
- has something valuable to say
- has some sort of merit in life.

BUT IT DOESN'T!

It is to be pitied.
It's a pathetic thing.
It's very sad.
It needs rest
and care
and nurturing.

It does not

need to be

in charge of

anybody's life.

And so you can address it with calm
and soothing words, as you would any
suffering person.

You don't let it run your life.
You don't let it sign on your
   bank account.
You don't let it arrange your
   calendar.
You don't even let it cook for
   you!

Are you with me?

STUDENT: I am with you. Sometimes I don't see that separation. Right now, right here in this room, it seems very clear to me.

GUIDE: I can give you the simplest of of all possible rules of thumb:
    Any time a voice is talking to
    you that is not talking with
    love and compassion,
    DON'T BELIEVE IT!

Even if it's talking about someone else, don't believe it. Even if it is directed at someone else, it is the voice of your self-hate. It is simply hating you through an external object. It can hate you directly by telling you what a lousy, rotten person you are, and it can hate you indirectly by pointing out
            what's wrong
                    out there.

If the voice is not loving,
don't listen to it,
don't follow it,
don't believe it.

NO EXCEPTIONS!

Even if it says it's "for your own good",
it is not. It's for its good, not yours. This
is the same as when parents talk to you
in a hateful tone of voice "for your own
good." It's for their good. It makes
them feel better. It does not make you
better. (And it does not make you
behave "better.")

Here are some outrageous things I
suggest about this. Any time you hear
the voice of self-hate, do something
for yourself that will make it crazy.
   Buy yourself a present.
   Sit down and read for pleasure.
   Take a long, hot bath.

STUDENT: Whatever it is that you can't let yourself do.

GUIDE: Yes. Whatever would be lazy and indulgent...

STUDENT: ... thoughtless, selfish...

GUIDE: <u>YES!</u> The move, the better. It can be as simple as going for a walk on a nice day. You just keep walking until the voice is still, until it is clear that it's not in control anymore. Then, when you're ready, when you're present, go back to your regular life.

Let's say that you sense you have been less than kind toward someone.

The voice of constructive criticism says, "That was pretty harsh. You're too sarcastic. You always have been. You better clean up your act before you alienate everyone."

This voice justifies itself by saying things like,

"I'm just trying to point these things out to you so that you'll be a better, kinder, happier person."

⇨

"Constructive criticism" is a scam run by people who want to beat you up. And they want you to believe
   that they're doing it
      for your own good!

Be suspicious of any voice
inside or outside
that says,

"THERE IS SOMETHING
WRONG WITH YOU."

This voice

DOES NOT LIKE YOU
and
IS NOT HELPFUL.

It is possible

that with the awareness that you have been unkind toward someone, you might realize, in a gentle sort of way,

"I don't want to do that. It doesn't feel very good."

And it's not that you've a bad person, or even that you shouldn't be that way; it's just that you don't want to be unkind because it hurts your heart.

When you are open to that awareness, you won't need to try to be different, for in that gentle approach,

you will already have changed.

COMMON WISDOM
that supports self-hate

- It is more blessed to give than to receive.
- You can't teach an old dog new tricks.
- The lyrics to "Santa Claus Is Coming to Town".
- You get what you deserve.
- The harder you try, the better you'll do.
- Two heads are better than one.
- Some things are just meant to be.
- If you are not the lead dog, the view never changes.
- Children should be seen and not heard.
- Do as I say not as I do.

ADD YOUR OWN:

-

-

-

-

~ CONFLICTING BELIEFS ~
that maintain self-hate

Patience is a virtue.
Strike while the iron is hot.

I am my brother's keeper.
Look out for Number One.

Neither a borrower nor a lender be.
Generosity is a virtue.

Carpe diem. (Seize the day.)
Save for a rainy day.

Be realistic.
Be imaginative.

Express yourself.
Control yourself.

ADD YOUR OWN:

Self-hate is

putting incredible pressure
on myself to be perfect

which causes me to make mistakes*
because I'm so stressed and overwhelmed
and miserable.

* It isn't actually possible to make mistakes.

STUDENT: I'm aware that I tend to focus on punishment and not notice reward. I seem to believe that punishment works and reward doesn't. I wonder what I get from having this belief.

GUIDE: What a good reason for doing things that are "wrong"; one can have all that punishment.

STUDENT: It seems I have an investment in misery.

GUIDE: Keep in mind that misery and egocentricity are synonymous. To be miserable is to be the center of the universe.
Now let's add the ingredient of feeling oneself innocent and yet punished. "I may have done something wrong, but it wasn't THAT bad. Surely I don't deserve THIS!"

Isn't that perfect? We even use our misdeeds to our own advantage. I've done something wrong, but I've turned it around so that I am the victim and should be compensated.

And egocentricity is usually right there with suggestions that could make up for this injustice.

Things like:

- ice cream
- not returning a wallet you find
- driving discourteously
- gossiping
- having an affair with someone else's partner

"After all, life owes me something."

SELF HATE
ACCOUNTING SYSTEM

In the self-hate accounting system:

- I add up everything I do.
  I subtract everything everyone
  else doesn't do.
- I add everything everyone else gets.
  I subtract everything I don't get.

— You get the picture. —

I am so far in the hole because all
I do is good things
        and all I get is bad things.

So . . .

... how can I not feel myself to be
a victim?

And why should I not try
to even things out?

And, of course,
what we fail to see is
that almost everyone
sees themselves as victims
and others as victimizers
so we continue
to victimize one another.

Who of us will stop?

SELF-HATE
AND THE
BATTERING CYCLE

We often think of the battering cycle happening between a man and a woman, but it can happen with any two or more people. In the form of self-hate, it requires only oneself.

In the classic situation, a man and a woman get together because they want to make their lives better. He will take care of her, and she will be supportive to enable him to take care of her.

After a while it stops working. The stresses of life push him to a crisis point, and he relieves his frustration by beating her. Then he feels good because his stress is relieved, but he feels bad because he beat his wife.

she feels good because she has been punished for letting him down, but she feels bad because her husband just beat her.

Then they get together and decide that this awful thing must never happen again, and they both feel better.

They have a plan. It's under control. "We won't make that mistake again. We'll do better. We'll be perfect."

And the stess begins to build again...

Addictive behaviors —
   whether it's food, alcohol, drugs,
   sex, smoking, work, relationships —
follow the same cycle.

FOR EXAMPLE:

The stresses of life begin to build, and
I reach for my addiction of choice. If
it's food, I head for the kitchen and
eat my way from one end to the
other.

I feel good because
the stress is
relieved. I have
kind of
anesthetized
myself, and the craving is calmed
But I feel AWFUL
         because I have
         just eaten a ton!

So I beat myself
until I'm convinced
that I've got a grip on it.

I see what happened.
It will never happen again.
I have a program.
I've got it right this time.
I'm going to do better.
In fact, I'll be perfect.

And the stress

begins to build...

THE BATTERING CYCLE

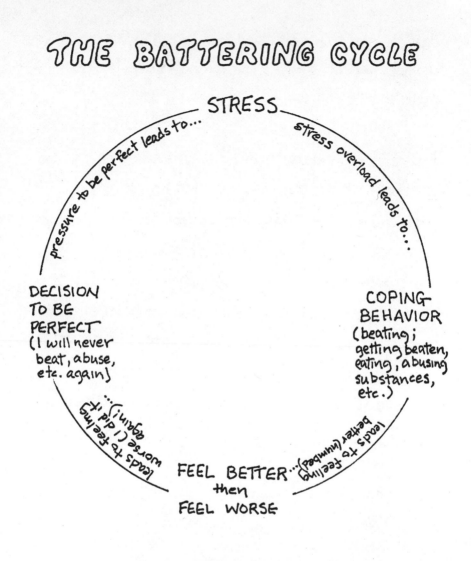

STRESS

pressure to be perfect leads to...

stress overload leads to...

DECISION
TO BE
PERFECT
(I will never
beat, abuse,
etc. again)

COPING
BEHAVIOR
(beating;
getting beaten,
eating, abusing
substances,
etc.)

leads to feeling
worse (I did it
again!)...

FEEL BETTER...
then
FEEL WORSE

...(feeling numbed)
leads to feeling better

This process can happen
- between two people
- within ourselves (between two parts
  or subpersonalities)

The conditioned belief that you must be perfect is the perfect setup for self-hate.

You believe that your choices are to be perfect or not to be perfect. But
EGOCENTRICITY SETS THE
STANDARD OF PERFECTION!
And since suffering, fear and self-hate are all egocentric, you can bet you are never going to meet that standard. If you did, if you met that standard,
what would self-hate beat you with?
What would egocentricity frighten you with?
And if you weren't frightened, how would you be controlled?

Egocentricity would have you believe that either it is in control, making you be who and how you should be, or you'll just be garbage.

The conditioned assumption is that if you
were to be just how you are,
you would be awful.

Self-hate
judgment
blame
punishment
rejection
are all for your benefit because they're
the only things keeping you from being
A TERRIBLE PERSON.
(HAVE WE MADE OUR POINT?)

Would you please risk it
and find out once and for all
how you are
WITHOUT the beatings and abuse?

I'm suggesting that you stop beating yourself. Many spiritual teachers suggest that hatred is not the answer. They say things about love, forgiveness, generosity and gratitude. They hardly talk about beating people and hating people and this sort of thing. All those people are saying, "Now, folks, this is the direction. This is really the way to go. If you really want to wake up and end your suffering and find joy and peace and bliss, this is the way to do it." And the response is, "Nah, I don't think so. I'm not going to do that."

So, here's the deal. If you were to, say for instance, find the willingness to stop beating yourself for just one day, and if you turned into a more hideous person than you are now, the next day you could beat yourself twice as hard and catch up.

I'm just suggesting that you might consider taking the risk.

≈ ♥ ≈

GUIDE: It takes a tremendous amount of courage to stop beating ourselves. I suspect it's not because we *really* think we'll be bad if we stop beating ourselves. I suspect it's because we don't want to come up against what egocentricity is going to do to us if we start taking control of our own lives.

If you decide that you are no longer going to be intimidated by the beatings of egocentricity, you will be immediately engaged in a life and death struggle because the moment that "stick" is taken away... think about it! If you aren't threatened with punishment, what will drive you to succeed? To make those phone calls? To make that list? To get through that list? What's going to happen if you don't do the thing you're supposed to do?

STUDENT: My life will go down the tubes. I'll be accused of being irresponsible. I'll lose that image I have of myself. People will see through me. I'll feel guilty.

GUIDE: It'll get so bad that you'll just die of guilt.

STUDENT: Eventually, I think that's what it comes to. If I don't do my work, and don't make money, then I won't be able to pay for my house, and I won't have any food. And, eventually, if you follow that along far enough, all those things on the list are designed to keep me alive. And, if I follow them back, if I don't do them, the ultimate consequence is death.

GUIDE: And that's what happens, isn't it? Do this task or die. (laughter) Even if it's get a haircut today. What if you found out that voice had no power over you at all? What if you didn't believe that you were going to die if you didn't do what it told you to do?

STUDENT: Well, I think I would do the next thing on the list. The belief is that I need the beatings. I need the fear of death to do all of these things. I believe it's that drive that keeps me going and keeps me working and doing things.

GUIDE: So, what would happen if you stopped believing the voices of self-hate? What would happen to you if you stopped the beatings?

STUDENT: I find that my worst beatings don't come about my list of things to do. They're about behavior, psychological kinds of things and emotional ways that I have learned I'm supposed to be, as if they are the laws of the universe. I must be polite in these circumstances. I must be nice or clever or whatever it is.

GUIDE: So, you come home after an evening out during which you've said something unfortunate. What would happen if you didn't respond to that?

STUDENT: Well, I have tried it. I've had some success, and it does seem to require terrific energetic awareness, every second. It takes a huge amount of being present. And it takes courage because it feels so much like it is the good person thing to do to scold myself for what I've done.

GUIDE: Yet, what you're describing is not scolding.

STUDENT: It's worse than that.

GUIDE: It's abuse. That's what you're really describing. And so, the good person thing to do is to be abusive. Pretty weird, huh?

STUDENT: There seems to be an element of not having control and/or giving up control. If I don't beat myself up, there's a feeling of spaciousness, and at the same time a terror of that spaciousness. Part of me wants more than anything not to be in control, to just go with the moment, to flow with the process. Another part clings desperately to control— wants to know what's going to happen, wants to like what happens, to influence what happens. But what comes out most for me is this one that's just terrified.

GUIDE: But not terrified of abuse, is fine with abuse, but is terrified of the lack of it, of the spaciousness.

STUDENT: Yeah. Not beating myself creates an oddly uncomfortable sense of freedom, total freedom.

GUIDE: Freedom and spaciousness, that's what's there. It's also a loss of identity because identity is maintained through this insanity we're describing. That's what keeps me at the center of the universe. That's what keeps the whole thing going. This underlying anxiety drives me to consume myself. As long as I'm doing that, there has to be a self to consume. If I learn to pay attention, to be present in the moment, I can see all of this happening.

If I am practicing meditation, I am growing daily, one hopes, more accustomed to spaciousness, to a feeling of freedom. I'm practicing coming back to the present, to center. I wander off; I drop it; I come back. Wander off... drop it... come back. Over and over I realize that nothing goes wrong; nothing happens to me. I'm perfectly fine.

If you're ever going to be free, you must be willing to prove to yourself that your inherent nature is goodness, that when you stop doing everything else, goodness is what's there. You'll never prove that to yourself as long as you're beating yourself, as long as you think the only thing making you a good person is beating yourself. At some point, if you're sincerely going to pursue spiritual practice, you must find the courage to stop beating yourself long enough to find out that who you are is goodness.

This is why we have a meditation practice: to learn to sit still with *whatever* is happening *There isn't anything in any of it. It's just stuff.* It's just what we're hooked into, what we're identified with, what we're clinging to in order to try to maintain this illusion of ourselves as separate beings, it's all that scrambling that we're conditioned to do. Something goes wrong, someone disapproves of us, or we disapprove of ourselves, and we go into high gear to try to make it right so that we can get everything put back together.

When we sit still in meditation, we don't scratch if we have an itch. Now, this drives people crazy. I've had people say, "This is demented. How could not scratching when you itch have something to do with spiritual practice?" It has everything to do with spiritual practice because it's that, "It itches, I *must* scratch" response that is at the root of most of our suffering.

But you can just notice that it itches (ah, itching) and not have to do anything about it. You can realize that you are having a conditioned response to a sensation. You don't have to take it personally. You don't have to respond to it.

If you once learn that you don't have to respond that way, you're free of it. You prove to yourself that you won't die and you won't go crazy and parts of your body won't fall off. You can just be there and be perfectly fine. Then something hurts and you can sit through that. It just becomes interesting. You're not resisting it any more. It's just kind of fascinating how it hurts there and pretty soon it hurts here, and then it doesn't hurt at all.

And then you think, "You know, my leg was hurting." You're sitting there quietly, breathing in, breathing out, and this helpful little voice says, "Wasn't your leg hurting a little while ago?" Suddenly, you're in pain again. So we learn to sit still with that. Or, maybe you're obsessing about something. The voice says, "You know, I can't sit here. I can't stand this. I've got to get up and ..." And you just sit there. You don't respond to it.

Maybe you become interested in obsession itself. (What is obsession? How do I do that?) Pretty soon you lose interest in that. You become bored with it because it's not making you <u>do</u> anything. Then, maybe you turn your attention to boredom... and you just sit there.

Eventually, it all begins to quiet down.

In the same way, when something happens in life, you no longer believe that you have to respond to it. You've sat still through so many "emergencies," so many "life and death issues," you no longer believe them. In not responding, the very energy, the force, the karmic conditioned force that is behind them, begins to have to feed on itself. It's no longer feeding on you because you're no longer participating in it. It has no fuel. And, eventually, it simply burns itself up. It simply burns itself away.

≈ ♥ ≈

STUDENT: Yesterday I was thinking that if I'm going to learn to love myself, I need to learn to love myself just the way I am. It occurred to me that even being overweight, I need to be thankful for this opportunity to love myself. It comforts me to think I might be this way for a reason and that reason might be to learn to love myself.

GUIDE: Yes. Even if you lost weight and had a "perfect body," but had not learned to love yourself, where would you be?

STUDENT: I would still be trying to improve myself, to fix the things that I think are wrong.

GUIDE: And all you would have done is to become acceptable enough to yourself that you can love conditionally, which is where we all are.

As long as you do it right, look a
certain way, act the way you should,
accomplish certain things, you'll be
lovable.
But can you be lovable
not meeting the standards?
Can you love this person who does not
meet the standards that you were
taught must be met before you can
be lovable?

Can you stop trying to change into who
you wish you were long enough to find
out who you really are?

You will never be able to improve
yourself enough to meet your standards.
Egocentricity will see to that. But the
moment you love
yourself, you are
completely changed.

Not wanting to be how you are

is one of the most

significant aspects

of self-hate.

We have been conditioned to believe that it's not okay to feel what we feel or think what we think or have the experiences we're having. As children, people didn't like us when we did that so they tried to change us. We've internalized that, and we've taken on that system ourselves. So now we're trying to change everything we don't approve of.

In acceptance, we don't want to change those things about ourselves. It's only in non-acceptance that we hope acceptance will mean that they change.

We can have
the full range of experience
that is our potential,
and we can enjoy it all.

If we move through and beyond that conditioning to change, then everything is available to us. If you're miserable, there's nothing really wrong with that, but if you're hating being miserable, then it's hell. If you're miserable and not hating it, you'll probably move through it pretty quickly.

Experiences do move along quickly when we're present. It's when we stop being present and get stuck in something that we can drag it out forever.

≈ ♥ ≈

We are never going to "get" something —
a philosophy,
a formula,
a fixed point of view —
that will make us forever different.

There is no secret
that will fix you.

(Remember, there is nothing
wrong with you.)

This is a lifelong process.
If you decide to learn to care
for yourself,
        to live your life
        in compassion,
you will be required to practice that
        until you die.

An internal relationship
must be worked on and maintained
just like an external relationship.

AND THAT'S GOOD NEWS!

When you fall in love with someone
you don't say,

"Oh, no, how long am I going
to have to love this person?"

When we're in love
we love
to love
that person,
and we hope
it will last
forever.

When you don't hate
yourself you won't

be chronically late
be chronically early
procrastinate
work compulsively
abuse substances
deprive yourself
depress your feelings
try to be perfect
worry too much
worry about worrying too much
depend on other's approval
believe your Judge
reject your Judge
punish yourself
overindulge yourself
pass up opportunities
be afraid of yourself
try to improve
try to improve others
etc.

We are responsible
for being
the person we've always wanted
to find.

We must become our own best friend.

We must learn
to give to ourselves
and
to receive from ourselves
unconditional love and acceptance.

It is not selfish.
It is the first
GIANT STEP
toward
selfLESSness.

We call people selfish
            when they WILL NOT give.
            But they CAN NOT give
            what they DO NOT have.

It's like asking a starving child to share
her food, and then making her feel guilty
for not wanting to.

            When we have enough
            we are eager to share.*

* What we <u>have</u>
and what we are able to <u>receive</u>
are two very different things.

THOSE WHO FEEL COMPLETELY LOVED ARE NOT SELFISH, THEY ARE LOVING.

What we're doing here is trying to scrape away the layers of stuff that we cling to instead of experiencing our intrinsic, inherent enlightenment. What we're seeking is there when we stop doing everything else. It's simply a matter of realizing what already *is*. It's not necessary for us to *do* anything.

We don't have to change.
We don't have to fix ourselves.
We don't have to improve.
We don't have to do it right.

It doesn't have anything to do with that. That's what we focus on instead of simply being here. That's why the self-beatings are so important to us. They are probably the single most effective method of avoiding awakening. That's why we have so much resistance to acceptance, because in acceptance there is nothing to do.

≈ ♥ ≈

We don't need to DO anything.

To sit still
in compassionate acceptance
is all that is required.

There is a small child inside each of us who
was taught to believe that bad things
happen, or will happen,
because s/he is bad.

As adults, when
we become aware of this child, we are
saddened and we feel the child's sadness.
We are conditioned to try to STOP the
sadness, to move away from the
experience.

The child doesn't need for
us to do that. S/He needs to know,
deep down inside, that it is absolutely all
right to be having that experience.
The child needs complete acceptance
for however s/he is in each moment.
And we, as adults, do too. That's what

we didn't get when we were little —
acceptance for however we are in
whatever moment.

The only response is compassion. Trying
to STOP, FIX or CHANGE is part of
the self-hating process.

Just stay with
the experience and

REALLY GET IT

that this is <u>sad</u>,
it's not wrong,
it's just hard,

it's hard to be a being.

How can we not feel compassion?

Of course, ego will jump right in there
and say, "Enough of this sadness. Let's
DO something about it."

That DO-ality will flip us right back into the bottom of the pot. I imagine a big stew pot of self-hate, and you just about crawl up to the top of the pot when you run into something that flips you right back in.

Usually this "something" is: trying to change what you are experiencing.

Criticizing yourself,
judging somebody else,
thinking you need to change something,
fix something,
DO something —

and you are right back
      in the bottom of the pot
            of self-hate

                                    again...

If you find it difficult to catch
the subtler self-hating processes
at work, it can be helpful to
sit in meditation.
One of the ways
we can see self-
hate in a meditation
practice goes something
like this:

You're sitting there,
        just breathing,
        paying attention,
        quiet, still.

You begin to notice that even
though all you are doing is
sitting silently and breathing,
a part of you is constantly
scanning, trying to find just
the thing that will
                pull you away
                from the stillness.

It says things like:

ACT STRONG AND CAPABLE

ALWAYS BE POLITE

FOCUS ONLY ON THE POSITIVE

MAINTAIN STRICT SELF-DISCIPLINE

This continues until something hooks you and your attention wanders. Soon you realize that you have been daydreaming / fantasizing / worrying / problem solving and you bring your attention back to the breath.

Now THIS is another perfect place to see self-hate at work

Your attention wanders.
You realize it
and come back to the breath.

Don't waste your time and energy
beating yourself up for having
wandered.

Just sit quietly in gratitude

for having returned.

Self-hate's greatest talent is self maintenance. It carries on a thorough, aggressive, sometimes loud, sometimes quiet, often subtle campaign to keep us in it's grip.

It would justify itself by claiming that it enables us to survive. That is a delusion.

We do not need to beat, punish, discipline, chastise, berate, and belittle ourselves and we never did. THE IRONIC TWIST IS THAT PUNISHING OURSELVES IS WHAT KEEPS US FROM SEEING THAT WE DON'T NEED TO PUNISH OURSELVES. If we can ever become aware and willing enough to break the internal battering cycle and NOT INDULGE IN THE BEATING we can begin to see how this is so. It takes courage and patience and faith in our inherent goodness.

PAINFUL THINGS COME UP NOT TO RUIN OUR
LIVES, NOT TO MAKE US MISERABLE,
NOT TO SPOIL OUR GOOD TIME,
THEY COME UP IN ORDER TO BE HEALED,
TO BE EMBRACED IN COMPASSION.

We hate its persistence, but once we have embraced it, we are grateful that it kept up the clamor.

≈ ♥ ≈

Self-hate is

having a new car
and never cleaning it.

I'll let myself have it,
but I won't take really good
care of it.

Self-hate is

eating the dessert I want

and feeling guilty the whole time.

Self-hate is

not asserting myself on an issue
that is important to me

ANIMAL RIGHTS   ENDING HUNGER   APARTHEID
RECYCLING   ABORTION
NUCLEAR ENERGY   HEALTH CARE   CRIME

then making a life-and-death issue
out of something trivial

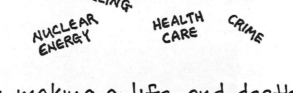

COLOR-CODED OFFICE FILES   MISPLACED CAR KEYS
DETERGENT BRAND   LOST SOCKS
TV CHANNEL   WHOSE TURN TO...   NOISY NEIGHBOR

which perpetuates the feeling
that I am a jerk.

STUDENT: Coming here today a voice was saying, "Nobody wants to hear what you have to say." Of course no one, including me, knew what I was going to say, but that doesn't stop that voice. Now that I'm here and I haven't said anything, the voice is saying "You're not participating. You should be talking."

GUIDE: So, whatever you're doing is wrong; whatever you did was wrong; and whatever you're going to do will be wrong.

Using a system like that to stay safe is like the cure being worse than the disease.

Self-hate is

"... torturing myself with 'fairness'.
I look at the amount of work I do
compared to my colleagues and say,
' I should be making more money.
It's not fair.' But I'm being paid for
the job I'm doing, and if I weren't
torturing myself with fairness, I'd
be happy with it. Instead, I stay
with this feeling that
I deserve more from
life than I'm getting.

Also, I'm paralyzed because I'm afraid
to ask for more money, afraid to make
waves, and I hate myself for being
afraid."

Self-hate coping behaviors
    make you feel better
    and
    make you feel worse
    at the same time.

All major addictions are like this.

        Self-hate
    is the ultimate addiction.

GUIDE: Self-hate is an addiction and a lot of self-hate is accomplished through other addictions.

I was talking to someone last night who had been sober for four and a half years and had gone out and had a drink. I told her that when she no longer hates herself, she won't need to do that. When you don't hate yourself, you don't want to mistreat yourself. It's as simple as that.

With an addiction like alcohol, there has to come a time when you sit at the kitchen table with a bottle in front of you, and you sit there until you know you're not going to drink. Like the movie *High Noon*, you've got to go out and face the Bad Guy. You may get lucky, or you may not, but you have to go out there for the showdown or pretty soon the bad guys are going to run the town. You can't hope that self-hate is going to get tired of beating you up and go away. Like blackmail, once the extortion starts, it's going to bleed you for everything you've got and then it's going to leave you for dead. It's not going to take your last dime and then leave; this isn't just turning off the faucet— it's ripping the plumbing out.

So do you want to take a chance with a confrontation, or do you want to just die a slow, lingering death? With the first choice you have a 50/50 chance; with the second, you have none. To stay with this analogy/parable/eulogy.... you actually have a much better than 50/50 chance, because as soon as you strap on your six-shooter and start walking down Main Street at high noon, there's not going to be anybody there.

STUDENT: Right. Nothing bears up under scrutiny. In fact, nothing shows up under scrutiny.

GUIDE: But if you're sitting quaking in hiding, you'll never make it to Main Street. As FDR said, "We have nothing to fear but fear itself." We are so afraid of being afraid, we are so afraid that we will be inadequate, that we won't prove to ourselves that we're not. The one who is projecting the inadequacy— in one of our previous scenes— says things like, "You think you're going to be a runner?" It's a different role, so it's sometimes hard to see that it's coming from the same source.

But who is invested in your being afraid? In maintaining an illusion of inadequacy? Do people who love you want you to be afraid? Want you to experience yourself as inadequate? Unworthy and undeserving? No, not at all.

Once we realize that fear is a process, we can get a handle on it. And there's nothing that's going to push you into this any faster than confronting the self-hate in the way that I've described, because terror will arise. Every time a hateful voice comes up and starts telling you something, you just sit on the couch and read a book, or go out and look at flowers, or take yourself out to lunch, or go to a movie.

STUDENT: Then terror arises?

GUIDE: Yes. Self-hate is terrified that you will make being kind to yourself a habit.

It comes down to this for me: None of my heroes (and all my heroes are religious types) ever says, "The important thing in the universe is to be at one with fear and inadequacy." OK? Nobody has ever defined God as "fear and inadequacy," and then said that is what you should strive for. And so, if I'm going to hold True Nature, Buddha Nature, God as the greatest value in life and then on a moment-by-moment basis choose the opposite of that, then what am I doing? This is the fundamental spiritual issue. How can I go beyond this fear in order to choose the wisdom, love and compassion?

STUDENT: Yes. How does one get beyond that?

GUIDE: For me, I go back to "putting the bottle on the table." I have times in my life of sitting on my cushion and holding onto it because that's the only way I can avoid screaming or suicide or madness as every bit of the conditioning comes up inside of me and says what it says.

St. John of the Cross talked about the dark night of the soul, and to me this is exactly what he is talking about. His image of it was God and the devil wrestling for your immortal soul. And isn't that what it feels like? And doesn't it seem, most of the time, like the devil is winning?

STUDENT: Yeah. It could even look like I'm on the devil's side!

GUIDE: Yes, and so for me— and this is where I depart from a lot of the rest of the world— I really don't believe for a minute that there is something more important than that which I am seeking. *I don't think there is anything more important!* I don't think money is more important; I don't think security is more important; or a good reputation; or being popular; or having people like me; or anything else. I don't think that there is anything more important than my True Nature. So if something is coming between me and that, I am going to sit still until it is no longer there. I am simply going to sit down and sit still and keep coming back to what I know is true, until there is nothing between me and that truth. I know when that is. We all know when that is. We all know that moment of oneness with our True Nature, the peace, the joy, the comfort. We know when that's there, and we know when it's not.

It's like discord in a relationship with someone I love. I am going to turn my attention to that until that lack of harmony is gone and peace, joy and comfort are back. I don't say, "I'll look at that later." I want to look at it NOW! I don't want to look at anything else until that's resolved, and I know the resolution of it is in here (points to heart). So I'm required to sit still with it.

≈ ♥ ≈

The process of socialization teaches us:

- to assume that there is something wrong with us
- to look for the flaws
- to judge them when we find them
- to hate ourselves for having them
- to punish ourselves until we eradicate them.

(⇧ This is what "good" people do.)

Socialization does not teach us:

- to love ourselves for our goodness
- to appreciate ourselves for who we are
- to trust ourselves
- to have confidence in our abilities
- to look to our Heart for guidance

(⇧ This would be "self centered.")

Self-hate is like quicksand.

Everything you do to try to get out
causes you to sink deeper.

Every place you step to try
to avoid the place you're in,
also pulls you down.

In quicksand,
if you cease struggling
you will sink more slowly.

In self-hate,
when you cease to struggle
(when you accept)
you are free.

STUDENT: This is a pattern of self-hate I've noticed. Lately I've been trying to say, "Okay, I have this need and I'm going to stand up for myself this time. I'm going to ask for what I want." So I do it, and my worst fears come true. People don't like what I said or did. My need is rejected. Then self-hate comes in and says, "I warned you!" But then another voice that it hasn't been possible for me to hear before says, "But you did it. That's the important thing this time. It doesn't matter what happened afterwards; you did it."

GUIDE: Yes, we see the self-hate patterns and we practice with them. They aren't going to stop, they're going to continue. And they're going to hit a level heretofore unimagined because when you start trying to break this stuff up, it will escalate. When you start picking away at the foundation of egocentricity, it's going to bring out everything in the world to defend itself. We can count on that. It's when things are hardest for us and compassion is most needed that self-hate is strongest.

Because if you could have compassion for yourself in a time when you really need it, can you imagine how the self-hate system would begin to shake and crumble? You can't have too many of those experiences without beginning to question whether all of this self-hate is actually accomplishing what it's saying it's intended to accomplish. That's why the answer is <u>compassion no matter what.</u>

Now, what we say is that we can have compassion as long as it's not a Really Terrible Thing we've done. But that's when we need the compassion most!

STUDENT: So if you've really blown it, done your worst, and all the self-hate voices come up, then the compassion needs to accept even those voices. . .

GUIDE: When we stop seeing them as powerful, when we see them instead as pathetic, as lost and hurting and misguided, how could we not have compassion?

STUDENT: Something that has made a difference for me in understanding acceptance is realizing that things don't have to change for me to accept them. If something is happening, all I have to do is acknowledge that, and that is accepting it. It's not as if my acceptance or non-acceptance can change whether it happens or not. It's already happening, and all I can do is acknowledge it.

GUIDE: I can't make any of this happen but I can show up and be available, and that's to me what sitting practice is— being constantly willing to show up and be available. Like having one's hands open to receive: There's no guarantee that you're going to get anything, but if anybody wants to give you something, you're ready.

STUDENT: I wouldn't say I'm consistent or disciplined about sitting. But being consistently willing to look at things and to use the world as a wall on which I can see my own projections, I can acknowledge that there are parts of myself that I don't like and I'm afraid of.

GUIDE: That's the crux of the whole thing because the basis of our practice is ending suffering, and at every moment we have the opportunity to see what in us is suffering. What is outside the realm of compassion? What is not healed? And we can bring that into the healing light of compassion by simply acknowledging it, accepting, it, allowing, it. This is the kind of person I am. This exists in me. I feel this, I do this. I have these thoughts. I have these tendencies. The conditioned patterns of suffering would have us hide those so that they continue to exist outside the healing light of compassion. And only to the degree that we can find the willingness to bring them into that light can they be healed.

In that way you can have all of you, instead of trying to put out only those things that egocentricity feels are acceptable. You can be, you can experience, you can have everything, just being who you are in the moment.

STUDENT: In spite of knowing how joyful it is to have that happen, it's still terrifying to find another aspect of myself that I hadn't seen before.

GUIDE: Yes, because egocentricity sees that as death. As long as there are those awful hidden things in you, self-hate can control your behavior. When you're willing to let everything come into the light of day, self-hate no longer has any power over you.

≈ ♥ ≈

If I could have compassion
(love myself)
for hating myself;

(!)

I would no longer be hating myself;

☆ I'd be loving myself ☆

and nothing about me
would need to change.

If the voices in your head are saying, for example, that you are a bad spiritual student, you're a bad meditator, you fidget, your mind wanders, this is one thing. At some point you could identify that as self-hate and let go of it. But if you start thinking what a good meditator you are, what a good spiritual person you are, how well you're doing, how much better your practice is than other people's practice, that's quite another thing. That's very difficult to let go once you are hooked.

It's helpful to develop a habit of not believing any of the voices. That way you can listen to any of them— listen but not believe. In the same way, you can sit around a dinner table with a group of people and they're all talking: you can listen to them, but you don't have to decide who is right and who is wrong. It's not necessary at the dinner table, and it's not necessary within yourself. You can just have the attitude of being present but not involved. The attitude of mind is one of, "Is that so?"

When you can have that attitude of mind with other people, it's a big step. When you can have it within yourself, you're moving toward freedom. Because as all this yakety-yak goes on, you think you have to figure out which is right and which is wrong— but the part of you who's trying to figure that out is the problem. That's the person who is confused, who suffers. When you can just step back there isn't anything to figure out, and there's nothing to believe. There's just being fully present in the moment.

The voices take us out of the moment and make us believe there is a world other than the present. The more they can get us involved in that belief, the more we're going to believe in the separate self, the more we're going to suffer. The less we believe, the less we are seduced, the more we're able to be in the present, and the less there is someone to suffer.

≈ ♥ ≈

Learn to be present.

Practice hearing the voices in your head without becoming involved and without judgment.

And take it on faith that any voice, internal or external, that is telling you that

SOMETHING IS WRONG WITH YOU
is not the voice
of your
Heart,
god,
True Nature.

The reason acceptance
   isn't more popular
      is that in acceptance
         there is nothing to do. *

* In acceptance there is nothing "wrong"
that needs to be changed, fixed, worked
on or otherwise improved.

And the simple,
astounding,
mind bogglingly amazing
FACT
is that as soon as you accept
yourself

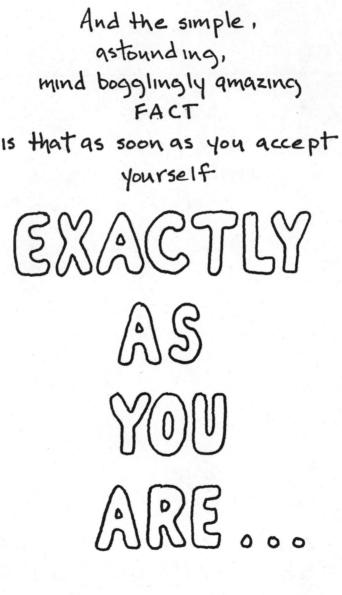

EXACTLY

AS

YOU

ARE ...

...all those
"character flaws"

ANGRY   STRESSFUL
    SELFISH
         AGGRESSIVE
    RECLUSIVE   SHY
SNOBBISH   DEPENDENT

 BEGIN TO FALL AWAY ←
            BECAUSE

those "flaws" have their
only existence
            in nonacceptance,
            in self-hate.

GUIDE: Nothing about how you are is a problem until you resist it. The problem comes into existence with resistence.

STUDENT: But what if I want to do something that's harmful?

GUIDE: Wanting to do something and doing something are two entirely different things. There's no need to act just because you have a feeling.

STUDENT: But what if I want to act?

GUIDE: Your questions come from a belief that you are inherently bad, and that if you don't control yourself, you'll be bad. When you realize that you are goodness and let yourself live from that, being harmful - intentionally harmful - would never occur to you.

If you take the
most frightening
thing in the world

and invite it in,

put your arms
around it,

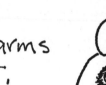

and sit still
with it,

what is left
to be frightened by?

Once I catch on to how this
self-hate process works,
I see that it goes on all the time,
everywhere.

Everyone does it.
This is just how we operate.

When I see this to be true,
self-hate ceases to be a private,
            secret thing I do
that proves I'm a bad person.

I can begin to take it less personally.

At some point,
now or later,
you're going to have to risk
Being You
in order to find out
who that really is.

Not the conditioned you,
not the you you've been taught
to believe you are,
who you _really_ are.

And this perhaps will be
the scariest,
the most loving,
the most rewarding
thing you have ever done.

If you are not becoming
kinder,
gentler,
more generous
and loving,
you are not doing this work.

If you are feeling more
burdened,
judgmental
and rejected,
you are doing self-hate.

We find this model to be a pretty accurate representation of how our conditioning toward fear and self-hate keeps us from knowing our original nature. →

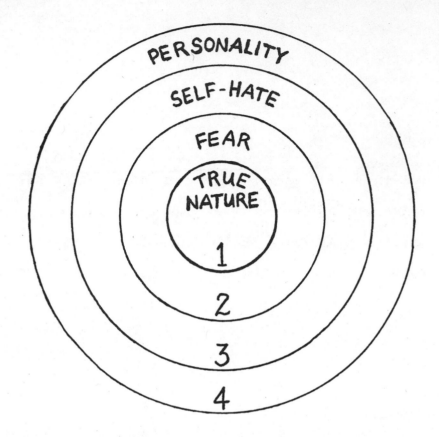

At the personality level (4), we have
our coping mechanisms, all our defenses,
our ways of getting by in the world. From
this level I might decide that I want
something more than life is offering,
that there must be something more
to it than meets the eye.

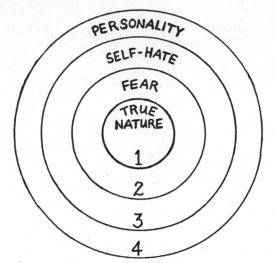

So I start working with the personality,
trying to improve it, fix it, figure it out.
I decide to get a different this or that,
a new mate, a new job, house, car. I
pursue personal growth, get into
therapy.

       I do all the things I think are
going to turn me into

                    the person
                    I should be.

There's nothing wrong with any of
this, it just doesn't work.

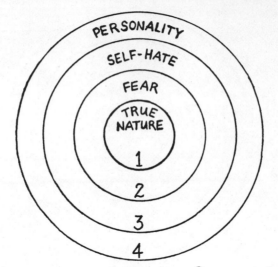

Finally, all these efforts fail and I decide to take the Big Plunge and begin some kind of spiritual practice, maybe a meditation practice, something that is designed to take me beyond the personality.

I begin the long, arduous journey to the center of my being.

The first thing I run into is self-hate (3). Now this is the layer that, thankfully, has been keeping the

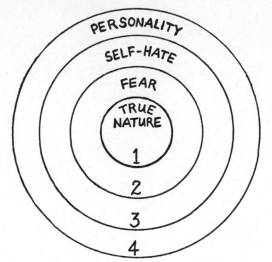

personality level from working! (Ours is a spiritual practice and does not have as its goal living a successfully egocentric life.)

So here I am at level 4 and I'm trying to become the perfect person, and level 3 is pointing out to me that it's not working. I'm going to improve myself and self-hate doesn't let me. Whenever I try to make a real beginning on this spiritual journey, self-hate will do anything it can to stop me and then beat me for stopping.

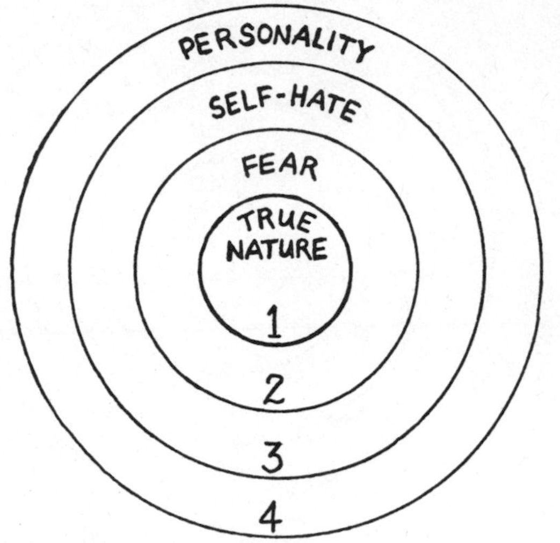
PERSONALITY
SELF-HATE
FEAR
TRUE NATURE
1
2
3
4

I'm going to start meditating
and self-hate stops me
and then beats me for stopping.

I'm going to start exercising
and self-hate stops me
and then beats me for stopping.

If I find the willingness to pay attention anyway, to struggle through all the self-hating voices, and I learn just to sit still through all of it and not be thrown off, the next level I encounter is fear (2).

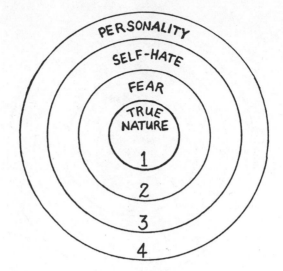

I've made it past the distractions, I'm being compassionate with myself, and then there's this little moment of silence...

What do I get? Fear. Big fear.
It says,
        "You're going to die!"
And I think,
            "How can that be the answer? I've gone through all this and THAT'S THE ANSWER?"

So I come back to level 3, self-hate,

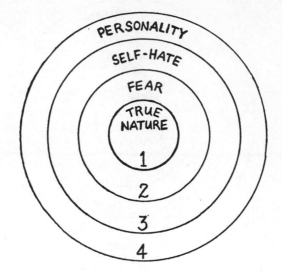

and I see that self-hate is pretty
handy because it works in both
directions:

    I can go from fear
    to self-hate, and
    I can go from personality
    to self-hate.

                 It's flexible.

I can hate myself for being afraid
and I can try to fix myself so that
I'm not afraid and I can be afraid of
the fear and I can hate myself for
being afraid not to hate myself...

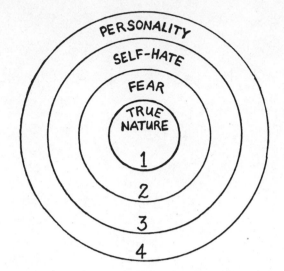

all designed to stop me from
getting to the center (1).

Perhaps, with patience and
willingness and experience, or just
plain old having suffered enough, I
eventually realize that this whole
process of going from
personality
↓
self-hate
↓
fear
↓
self-hate
↓
personality

and back again, has been exactly what
I needed to be doing to learn what
I needed to learn. I realize that
    every step
        I have taken
            has been
                on the Path.

Perhaps I realize that it has all been
happening perfectly and that True
Nature (!) was
        never inaccessible,
        never out of reach,
        always present,
        always guiding me.

There never was anything wrong.

                    I just didn't know it.

Egocentricity is invested in convincing you that you are an awful person — that deep down inside you there is some Horrible Thing. Why? Because it stays in charge that way.
It can just say

and you'll jump back into line and do whatever it says.

But you can call its bluff simply by saying,

"BRING OUT THE HORRIBLE THING. SHOW IT TO ME!"

And you can say,

" Don't worry. I'll keep it to myself. I'll keep it hidden. I won't tell anyone. Okay?"

But
egocentricity
can't do that.

And the more it cannot
show you the
Horrible Thing
the more it will dawn on you that
MAYBE IT DOESN'T EXIST.

MAYBE THERE ISN'T A
"HORRIBLE THING"
INSIDE OF YOU.

Ego begins to scramble at this point because power is shifting away from it—

and shifting to that part of you who is able to step back from ego and carry on this kind of dialogue with it,

that can begin to stop believing that there is something wrong with you —

the part of you
that is beginning
to be free.

I maintain
my identity
by not looking at myself.

This system, this identity, cannot
hold up under scrutiny. Nothing can.

So...

    right before I begin to see myself,
my conditioned identity, ego goes on
the defensive and the voices start:

    I'm bored.
    This is stupid.
    I don't need this.
    I can't do this.
    This doesn't work for me.
    I've got too much to do.

                etc.

It can sound as if we see egocentricity
   as an enemy,
                     but we don't.

Gandhi talked about his political
   opponents as teachers,
   for to have worthy opponents
   is a blessing.
                     They will force you
            to be the best that you are.

      That's the spiritual gift
      that egocentricity is for us.

Regardless of
what you were
taught to believe,
there <u>never</u> <u>was</u>
anything wrong
with you.

GUIDE: Okay, let's hear some self-hate. Answer this: What is wrong with you?

GROUP: Everything... I can't figure out what is wrong... I can't get it right... I'm never serious... I'm ungrateful... I'm critical and judgmental... I'm hell-bound... I'm angry... I'm never going to get what I deserve... I'm not a team player... I'm a wimp... I'm closed... I can't be trusted... I'm a phoney... I'm lazy and self-indulgent... I'm careless... I'm too serious... I'm a coward... I can't get with the program ... I'm never satisfied... I don't pay attention... I talk too much... I'm too slow ... I'm a quitter... I don't think enough... I can't keep up... I'm not good enough... I'm selfish... I'm mean... I'm unfriendly ... I'm unworthy... I'm unlovable... I'm dishonest... I'm proud... I always have to be in control... I can't talk right... I'm stupid... I'm out of control... I'm too emotional... I'm too sensitive.

GUIDE: As you were answering, I watched people get littler and littler. You were taking a quick trip back to childhood. The voices changed, the body language changed, the energy changed. Suddenly, I was sitting in the room with a bunch of very small children. They are very dear.

Egocentricity uses

SELF-IMPROVEMENT
as
SELF-MAINTENANCE.

As long as
you are concerned about
improving yourself,

you'll
always have
a self to improve.

Self-hate encourages you to judge,
then it beats you for judging.

You judge someone else and it's simply
self-hate projected outward,
                          then you
get to use it back on yourself
                          when you
beat yourself for judging!

                We call this,
        "Heads you lose, tails you lose."

STUDENT: Belief in fairness is such a setup for self-hate.

"If life were fair, if things were balanced the way they should be, this wouldn't be happening to me." It's easy to go from there to, "I must have done something wrong." It's that old "why do bad things happen to good people?" I guess there aren't bad things and good people, just things and people.

GUIDE: And that's frightening, isn't it? Because it means that we have no control. If anything can happen to us in spite of all our best efforts to make things go the way we want, where does that leave egocentricity? One of ego's threats is, "If you don't do exactly as I say, something awful is going to happen to you."

If you believe this threat...

the worst thing that can happen to you

HAS ALREADY HAPPENED!

STUDENT: What is this "worst thing"?

GUIDE: Belief in inadequacy. Believing that you are not equal to your life. Turning away from your True Nature, your Heart, god.

It's really quite miraculous, in the face of all our conditioned fear, to be willing even to consider sitting still with ourselves. We work and work to uncover the layers of our conditioning, and when we see what we've uncovered, our reaction is, "Oh, no, not that! I don't want to see that." What did we think we were going to see? We must remember that this is the layer of "stuff" between the one who is seeking and that which is sought. It's what keeps me from ME. We have been taught to hate it and fear it so that we'll be too frightened and disgusted to look at it. It knows that if we ever do— if we ever get back to our unconditioned selves— *the jig is up*! Getting back to who we really are means no more illusion of separateness, no more egocentricity. That's why it's so hard and why almost no one ever does it. Egocentricity is very powerful and very clever and very determined, because it thinks it is fighting for its life.

So, it looks worse and worse the deeper we go. That is why it's critical to learn to sit still and believe nothing that the voices say to you, that's why it's so crucial to find compassion.

≈ ♥ ≈

If the voice is not speaking compassionately to you, it has nothing to tell you.

Do not confuse
NICE AND POLITE
with
compassionate.

A compassionate person may be
what we call nice and polite, but
compassion does not try to be
nice and polite.

Nice and polite
come from conditioning.

Compassion
comes from the Heart
and
our shared connectedness.

STUDENT: I've found that a lot of my reluctance to do certain things in the practice comes from self-hating attitudes. For example, if I realize I am saying bad things to myself, it seems phony to make myself be compassionate by saying something good. But I'm finding that just making the effort is often helpful. Recently I'd been feeling crabby and not grateful, and just the mechanical act of writing "thank you" was enough to help me find the sense of gratitude. I could say that that was phony and stupid, but it worked.

GUIDE: The voice saying it's phony is terrified that you'll find out how sincere you are.

STUDENT: It's okay to just pretend you like yourself, to go through the motions of embracing yourself, even if it feels false or stupid. I figure that as long as I'm still centered in my head, I might as well find compassion up there, as an intellectual thing, until I can find it in my heart.

STUDENT: St. Teresa of Lisieux taught to go to the experience of gratitude within, and I've always assumed she meant fake it if it wasn't there. I often "act as if" and as soon as I do, I feel a real change.

GUIDE: Because it's <u>not</u> phony. You are acting the way you really are, according to your True Nature, and that gets beneath the self-hate.

≈ ♥ ≈

Student: I was at a conference where we were asked to sit in meditation for an hour each morning and it was mentioned that if you hadn't sat before, you might have various physical sensations, even nausea. I had never meditated before, but I wanted to do everything right, so I sat every morning. I was pregnant at the time, and through every sitting, I thought I was going to throw up. But since I knew to expect that kind of sensation, I kept sitting, and I made up my mind to stick it out even if I did throw up or if I passed out. What I learned was that I was able to get through it by staying with every single breath. And that experience showed me that the internal voices weren't right. They were saying, "You can't do this, you're going to be sick." But it wasn't true, even the physical cues I was getting. That was an extremely valuable experience. Later when I was in labor, it was true again: As long as I stayed with every breath, I was all right. And that showed me where freedom is.

GUIDE: Yes. If you went to another conference now and had a friend with you, say, and she was sitting those hours each day, even though she'd never sat before, you might be tempted to say to her, "I hope you know what a great thing it is that you are doing. It's really hard, and you're doing it." That's the kind of thing we'll say naturally to somebody we really care about, but we don't say to ourselves. But we could. We could even go beyond telling ourselves that it's okay to have our thoughts and feelings and risk something really compassionate like, "That was really good. I'm glad you did that. You're a good person. I like you." It's so funny to me that with that kind of recommendation, people say they're afraid of becoming egocentric and self-indulgent. But we already are!

≈ ♥ ≈

STUDENT: I've found it very helpful in meditation to tell myself that I love myself. At first it felt sort of phony and ridiculous, but I decided to keep at it, and the results have been amazing. Sometimes I've been in really terrible mental states, and the idea of loving myself will come up all by itself. It's brought me to tears at times because the compassion is really there. And because I've practiced verbalizing it to myself, those words will just arise.

GUIDE: The fact that we see it as corny or phony tells us that egocentricity is doing the judging. From a centered place, you would never see loving yourself as corny or phony. Only ego would add those labels. Calling it phony is self-hate; it's ego trying to get you to believe that loving yourself is an experience that you don't know. That's why I like this process of reassuring myself that I do love myself.

An example of self-love and acceptance in action could be something like this: Let's say that I've identified that I'm afraid. I could say, "I am a brave and courageous person.," but that's not going to do any good. Or I could say, "It's okay to be afraid," and begin to focus on what this fear is. "What is fear? What does it feel like? Where does it happen in my body? What do I say to myself when I'm afraid?" Then I may go ahead and do the thing I'm afraid of, and then I can ask, "At what point does the fear arise? How does the fear stop me from doing this thing? Can I feel the fear and do it anyway?" So, you see, there's somewhere to go with it. If it's okay to be afraid, all my options are open.

Am I afraid all the time? No. Well, when am I afraid? What exactly am I afraid of? If I'm trying to hide the fear, repress it, not let myself know that I have it, it can become a weapon for self-hate because suddenly I am just a frightened, fearful, whining, needy, cowardly person. But if I'm just afraid, and that's okay, that's an open doorway that I can go through.

It's not the fear, it's the attitude toward fear. To believe that I shouldn't be afraid of high places doesn't help if I really am afraid, and to pretend I'm not when I'm in danger is not intelligent, not taking care of myself.

If I allow the fear to go on inside and say to myself, "Yes, this is happening," there is a belief that it will go on forever. That's where we have to take the leap of faith. Just be still with the fear as it's happening and experience it for what it is and allow it to be healed within that acceptance.

≈ ♥ ≈

Fear is very dramatic.
It tells very plausible stories.
It makes strong feelings in your body.
It is the primary support of egocentricity.
It is egocentricity.

Ego is fear, and
ego is everything it then does to
    manage,
    control
    and avoid that fear,
    that experience of itself.

(It says," I'll protect you. I'll keep you safe.")

Ego spends enormous amounts of time
and energy pretending

                    to avoid itself!

Pay attention.

Self-hate is slippery. It will
even say things to you like,

"You shouldn't believe the
voices of self-hate. If you
are still believing them,
there really is something wrong
with you!"

It may be true that you make sacrifices,
but that doesn't make you good;
it just means you make sacrifices.

It may be true that you are accepting,
but that doesn't make you good;
it just means you are accepting.

It may be true that you are responsible,
but that doesn't make you good;
it just means you are responsible.

It may be true that you meditate,
but that doesn't make you good;
it just means you meditate.

We label these behaviors good
and then continue to do them
in order to support self-hate.
Perhaps
doing in order to be good is what keeps
you from realizing that you are already
good.

It may be true that you gossip,
but that doesn't make you bad;
it just means you gossip.

It may be true that you tell lies,
but that doesn't make you bad;
it just means you tell lies.

It may be true that you are impatient,
but that doesn't make you bad;
it just means you are impatient.

It may be true that you are sarcastic,
but that doesn't make you bad;
it just means you are sarcastic.

We label these behaviors bad
and then continue to do them
in order to support self-hate.
Believing
that what you do determines who you
are could be the real reason for continuing the behaviors, not stopping them.

It's a lose / lose game with self-hate.

If I feel good
I have to pay the price
because it's not really okay to feel good.

If I feel bad
I have to pay the price
because it's not really okay to feel bad.

STUDENT: I've heard you say that it's not possible to make mistakes. I'm having some difficulty understanding this. Would you say move about it?

GUIDE: Whatever it is that I'm doing, if I pay attention to it, I'm going to benefit. I'm going to learn something.

Look at your son, Evan, learning to walk. At what point should he have considered himself a failure and given up? All of the times he pitched over on his head or fell back on his bottom? Those were not successful from the definition of walking, yet they were not unsuccessful either. They were just part of the process of learning to walk.

If we want to wake up
and end our suffering,
(and if we are paying attention
to how we cause ourselves to suffer),
we are going to learn
from everything that happens.

For example,
I am going along in life working diligently
toward something, and it doesn't go the
way I want it to go.
                    If I am willing to
pay attention, not-getting-what-I-
want is very helpful.

   "Why didn't I get what I wanted?"
   "Why wasn't I in control?"
   "What went wrong?"
   "Who's to blame?"
   "What should I have done differently?"
   "Maybe I should try harder."

Well, now, there's a classroom for you!

Failure, making mistakes...the person who is agonizing over "should I take that job in Hoboken," as if transportation only goes in one direction. If you take the job and that's not where you want to be, you're doooooomed to stay there forever. It's not possible to say "oh, I don't like Hoboken," and leave.

It becomes life and death, all or nothing.

This reminds me of early Ram Dass with questions like
   "Should I cut my hair?"
   "Should I lose my virginity?"
   "Should I read Meher Baba?"
For us I suppose it would be
   "Should I read Rajneesh?"
(And, of course, the answer is: RISK IT.)

But the attitude of mind that is focused on this sort of thing
                    has already failed.

It's like the fear of making a mistake.
You've already made it.
You're already in as bad a place as
you can be in. ————→ Everything
after that is getting out.

This kind of information is not well
received by self-hate/egocentricity
because what would it beat you with
   if it weren't possible to fail?
   if there were no such thing
      as a mistake?
   if you couldn't do it wrong?
What would there be to beat yourself
over? And if there were nothing to
beat yourself over, where would the
control come from? What would
maintain the fear? What would maintain
the anxiety and
the inadequacy?
And the questions
that follow
those are:

WHO
AM I
NOW?

What would maintain egocentricity?
How would you know who you are?

It is only the illusion of a separate
self who could believe that it is
possible to make mistakes.
Because,
in fact,
there isn't anything going on
other than what is.

It is only in some imaginary parallel
universe where this could happen,
or this could happen,
that we get that kind of alternative.

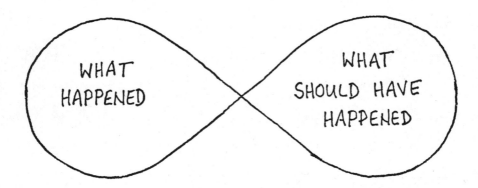

As far as I know, it is only when we hold the notion that
> something happened
> <u>this</u> way,
> but it should have happened
> <u>that</u> way
that we can say, "Well, I had <u>this</u> experience, but <u>that</u> is the one I was supposed to have."

I don't think so.

STUDENT: From the perspective of the part of me who believes in failure, none of what you're saying makes sense, and yet, what you're saying makes sense.

GUIDE: That's why, when we look at these issues, it is very helpful to come back to center, the present moment, to look at them because egocentricity is <u>invested in failure</u>.
> The payoff?

AS LONG AS YOU FAIL, YOU GET TO KEEP TRYING.

So you have to do it again. "I don't have it quite right so I have to do it again."

STUDENT: How could that be a payoff?

GUIDE: It maintains egocentricity. The whole universe is hinged on:

"Will I succeed?"

And I will say again what I have said so often. The reason acceptance is not more popular is that in acceptance there is nothing <u>to</u> <u>do</u>. Egocentricity <u>is</u> doing.

Non-acceptance
is always
suffering,
no matter
what you're
not accepting.

Acceptance
is always
freedom,
no matter
what you're
accepting.

A DEFINITION OF SUFFERING

The constant process
of trying to get and hold on to
that which we like,

and

the constant process
of trying to avoid and eliminate
that which we do not like.

Whatever is struggling

or discontent

or suffering

or afraid

IS that which needs

to be accepted.

Life is very short.

We do not have time
to be frightened.

We do not have the luxury
of allowing fear
and hate
to run our lives.

THIS
IS IT!

We're tense, stress-filled, in order to control life. We tense up, hold on tightly, and feel that
      we're making something happen
         (what we want),
or keeping something from happening
         (what we don't want).

If, in fact, by tensing up
we could control life,
we'd be foolish not to.

However, what we know is that being tense, being filled with stress, does <u>not</u> enable us to control life.

        Aren't we then
          quite foolish
       to maintain the tension?

                Because . . .

with this tense / no control situation
we have two problems :
   1) tension / stress
   2) no control over life.

In a no tension / no control situation
we would have only one problem :
   1) no control over life
   which can be experienced as
         frightening
         or
         freedom.

We have no control but we think we
<u>should</u> have.

Letting go of the illusion of control
will not make you more vulnerable,
it will make you more relaxed
                    peaceful
                    open
                    receptive
                    joyful
                    calm.

Children have no control and don't
think they should have.

"Yes, but look what happens to kids!"

Life is life with or without the illusion of control. Children feel the pain of life. Pain and suffering are not the same thing. Suffering happens when we are taught to believe that what is happening to us is wrong, a mistake, and we should have prevented it.

We <u>learn</u> to think of life as reward and punishment.

- I'm good. Good things happen to me. I get what I want.
("Eat your peas then you can have pie.")

- I'm bad. Bad things happen to me. I don't get what I want.
("You didn't do your homework. No television for you tonight.")

As adults,

We turn it around:
   I didn't get what I wanted;
   something bad happened;
   I must have done something wrong;
   I'm being punished for being bad.
("My husband was killed. I'm being
punished for being a bad person.")

And do not believe for a second
that we are saying
that the abuse of children
is not a problem.
            Of course, we are
not saying that.
            We've asking you
to see that continuing to practice
self-hate will not prevent child abuse.

            ⇨

Self-hate won't prevent the
abuse of little children who
are currently in little bodies,
            and
it won't prevent the abuse
of little children who are
currently in big bodies
(such as your own).

THE ONLY WAY WE ARE EVER
GOING TO STOP THE ABUSE OF
CHILDREN IS BY CEASING TO
BELIEVE THAT PUNISHING
PEOPLE MAKES THEM GOOD.

You cannot be nonviolent
if there is any part of you
that you are in opposition to.

You are not truly serving
if there is any part of
yourself to which you will not
extend compassion.

Your love will always be conditional
as long as you are excluding
any part of yourself from it.

Suffering / Pain cannot be healed
through self-hate - only through
compassionate acceptance.

If we accept,
if we open ourselves,
life will transform us.

If we resist,
if we try to run away,

the pain and the suffering are
reinforced - and we condition ourselves
again to suffer.

When we embrace,
the pain wears the suffering away.

If we can be willing and patient
life will work its
magic on us.

Little by little, all that is not compassion
will be stripped away,
burned away from us.

The pain of the suffering of holding
onto the conditioning, the beliefs,
the fear; will become so great that we
will let go.
And each time we let go,
we find in place of the suffering peace,
relief, ease and a growing sense of
gratitude and compassion.

STUDENT: I wake up in the night afraid of dying. I don't know what to do.

GUIDE: Meditating will take care of it for you. You will actually be able to experience what you are labeling fear. What is fear actually? Well, I'm afraid I'm going to die. You are going to die, that's true. Are you dying in this moment? Not so that it shows. Is it an experience you're having, or is it an idea that you're holding onto? What would that sensation be without those beliefs, those labels, without that conditioning? You wake up, everything is fine. A thought comes through, the fear follows it, then the voices kick in, and you're off to the races. There was nothing going on before that. How did you get there? What happened?

STUDENT: There were times when I would stay awake all night.

GUIDE: And believed every bit of it. So, you begin to see how that kind of process has served a purpose in your life. Now, the purpose may be no more complex than it perpetuates self-hate. It keeps you down. It keeps you terrified. It keeps you stuck. It keeps you safe. You start to take a risk, you feel the icy hand around the spine at 3:00 A.M., you knock off that risk-taking. Just get back to that safe place. Start doing all of those behaviors that make egocentricity feel in control and feel safe. Narrow that world down. Do what you're supposed to do. Beat yourself mercilessly and then maybe you'll be all right.

Through coming here and through paying attention in your meditation, you begin to suspect that what's <u>really</u> going on is a process that has nothing to do with what you <u>think</u> is going on. You begin to see that there are certain times when these patterns happen. You begin to notice that they, in fact, are patterns. You're no longer believing them. You're bringing it back closer and closer to the sensation that's actually triggering it. And you realize that there is no such thing as fear.

≈ ♥ ≈

Beginning to wake up.
Beginning not to take it personally.
Beginning to see that life
                    isn't anyone's "fault."

It just is
and you just are
and it's all just fine.

GUIDE: All of this psychological work that we do is, to me, wonderfully helpful, but it's useless without the sitting practice. Now, the sitting practice is not useless without the psychological aspect. You could just sit down and face a wall and eventually you would understand all this. It's all available without having any intellectual understanding of it. The two together are a really solid program for ending suffering. But most people want to have only an intellectual understanding and then make that work for them. But it's like having an intellectual understanding of riding a bicycle. It's great when you're sitting in the living room with a book reading about it, but when you are flying down a hill, it doesn't help. The only thing that's helpful is doing it, practicing.

In our sitting practice, we go to that place of inherent goodness, we find that deep sense of well-being within ourselves, and we become friends with that. We go there, and we see that being there is wonderful. For the periods of time that we're there, all the problems fall away, everything falls into place. And then we leave that and go get caught up in something. And we come back. That's why I talk about, rather than taking our spiritual practice into daily life, we bring our daily life into our spiritual practice. We're creating a circle of compassion, and we keep bringing the events of our life into it. If I am troubled about something, upset about something, I bring it into that still place, and there's peace there. It just resolves itself. It dissolves. And then I get caught up again, my mind takes off, I go into the conditioning, and I'm miserable again. And then I come back. I practice coming back here (indicating center), going out, getting miserable, coming back here. Eventually I get to the point where when I look at being here in the place of compassion, or being out there caught up in self-hate, there's just no question about it. I don't want to be out there caught up in self-hate. It's not that I'm pushing that away; it's not that I'm saying I'm a bad person for doing that. It's just that I look at it, I realize what's going on, I want to come back here.

≈ ♥ ≈

The benefit of working to see and let go of self-hate is that you cease to be afraid of yourself, and you find a greater willingness to sit down and be still with whatever is there inside you. When you stop believing the voices of self-hate, you will notice a curious thing— emptiness, a hole inside yourself. Instead of distracting yourself and trying to fill it up, if you become curious about how to sit down and be <u>with</u> the emptiness, it is a very wonderful thing.

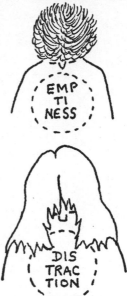

When we try to fill up that hole with distractions, that's what really leaves us feeling empty. That emptiness is full of suffering; it's a narrow, closed experience. The other emptiness is an open, spacious feeling, and yes, ego is uncomfortable with it because ego doesn't exist there. If we can let ourselves get used to that spaciousness, it is a wonderful experience.

≈ ♥ ≈

In the present
we can embrace the past
and free the future.

If the future is not freed
to be the present it is,
our present will always
be lived in the past.

GUIDE: I asked people if they had had a pleasant evening, and many indicated that they had not. So could we hear from some of the victims of post-self-hate-workshop self-hate?

STUDENT: When I left here, I felt a sense of gratitude. "Here's the road to freedom, and I forgot, and it's very helpful to be reminded." Then I watched myself use that information against myself. This was the situation: Part of me is very indecisive, and in trying to decide whether I should spend the evening doing A or B, she became totally flustered and just wanted someone to tell her what to do. Then another voice said, "That's duality. The answer is not to do it." And then another judging voice said, "What you need is compassion, and you're not giving it to yourself." So self hate took everything I learned yesterday and plugged it into the self-hating system.

I was left with this indecisive person who was suffering horribly, and yet another voice said, "You're just maintaining egocentricity." Afterwards, I could see that it was that voice that was maintaining egocentricity; the person who was miserable was just miserable. And I wasn't doing anything to help her; I was accusing her of doing it wrong.

Finally I cried and that seemed to release something. But I can see why people would stop paying attention. You start to see all this stuff, and it would be easy to decide that it's just too much.

GUIDE: And who would decide that except self-hate? Self-hate doesn't decide it's "too much" when it's beating you up— only when you have become aware and are seeing what has just happened to you. Doesn't that timing make you a little suspicious? If it's really too much, then stop beating yourself for being who you are. Isn't that where the misery comes in? So what if you have trouble making a decision? So what if you want someone to tell you what to do? So what if it's duality? So what if you're maintaining egocentricity? Would any of it be a problem if you hadn't been taught to believe that how you are is wrong? Will anybody die or even have something awful happen to them as a result of how you are ? No. So how do we justify all this violence? Someone has a hard time deciding between A and B. Should we kill her? Is she not fit to live? Or is it enough that she is simply beaten until she doesn't care if she lives? Can you see how insane this system is? How could violence and hatred improve anything? I would encourage you to risk the horrors of indecision and compassion.

I don't see grownups in all this. I just see little children, because that's how most of us feel inside. I picture this child who doesn't know whether she wants the red bucket of the blue bucket. The truth is, she wants them both. They're both really pretty and she likes them equally so she can't make up her mind. What she doesn't know is that in this world you only get one because getting both makes you selfish.

What's going to help her out here? How about if we start yelling at her about making up her mind? About how if she doesn't decide soon, she's not going to get either one? Would it help if our voices sound angry and our faces are red and we grab her by the arm and shake her? No. And yet how many children are "taught" in that manner?

Not knowing whether you want red or blue does not make you a bad person. Those things have nothing to do with each other. But isn't it hard to see that? We've been taught that everything in life makes you either a good person or a bad person. But it's not true, and it never was.

≈ ♥ ≈

All of life's conflicts are between

letting go
or
holding on

opening into the present
or
clinging to the past

expansion
or
contraction.

The Path of Patient Effort

Once upon a time there was a student who came faithfully to Zen retreats, but always in the grips of the belief that she was a Bad Meditator. At every retreat she agonized about this, and every time she said the same things: "I can't meditate. I sit on the cushion and I think about things, I daydream, I write books, I fidget. I just can't do this." And the teachers would say, "That's all right. Just keep showing up. Sit there. Pay attention when you can." Retreat after retreat, the same thing went on.

After five years, suddenly the Good Meditator showed up at a retreat. There was nothing to fight against any longer, and the part of the student who wanted more than anything to meditate was finally able to come to a retreat. Now, the Good Meditator was the one who had been bringing the student to every retreat all along, and taking whatever meditation time it could get. Self-hate told her, endlessly, what a bad meditator she was. But the Good Meditator patiently stayed with it, and finally the student was able to see that part of herself.

Moral of the story: No matter what anybody says, don't give up on yourself.

≈ ♥ ≈

Acceptance
is not only the path to creativity,
it is creativity.

Until you accept
nothing new can be,
you will have only the past.

If you want a new world,
accept the world as it is.

If you want a wholly new world,
accept it wholly.

When the Buddha wanted to find out how suffering happened and how to end it, and discovered that no one could tell him,

his response was to find out for himself.

It is possible for each of us to do this, although almost none of us wants to.

We think it's too hard. We
would rather focus on

what's (wrong) with us

and why we can't do anything
about it.

We don't want
   to take care of ourselves

         because

that means giving up the wish
   to be taken care of
   by someone else.

"I want my mother to do it.
She should have done it
but she didn't. I'm going
to stay stuck right
here until..."

Until what?
Until she does it?
But she can't do it.
And she never could.

Again, we need to consider this:
If we can't do it
how could somebody else have done it?

"Well I could do it now if she had
done it then."

No.
That's a scam run by
egocentricity
designed to keep you stuck.

It is time to cut out

the middle man.

Or woman.

LOVE · CARING · COMPASSION · KINDNESS
GENTLENESS · PATIENCE · UNDERSTANDING

We look for things that were done
to us because that makes us
the victim.

Then things are not
our fault; we don't have to
take responsibility.

We can point to all these

☞ REASONS ☜

that we are how we are.

☞

We can also say,

Yes, this did happen to me, and my parents did it to me because their parents did it to them and so on down the line.

And if I can't stop doing it to myself,

how can I expect them to have stopped doing it?

They weren't aware any of this existed. They were just being good parents

in the same way they were parented.

ALMOST NOBODY WANTS TO GROW UP.

Taking responsibility
is not
taking blame.

It's not your fault.
It's not someone else's fault.
It's not anyone's fault.

"FAULT" misses the point.

This is how it is.

This is your best opportunity
to turn it around.

There will always be future opportunities,
but why not use this one? ➡

– paraphrase of an old Zen story –

One hot summer afternoon, the monastery cook, an elderly monk, was spreading mushrooms on a mat to dry in the sun.

A young monk saw him and asked, "Why is an old man like you doing such hard work in the heat of the day?"

The old monk replied, "If not me, who?
If not now, when?"

– paraphrase of another old Zen story–

A woman went to a Zen monastery. She was so thrilled to be there – such a holy place, a place of enlightenment.

The first sitting period, she walked mindfully up the steps of the meditation hall. As she was preparing to bow deeply before entering, she noticed a shocking thing. There, at the top of the steps, was a bucket of filthy wash water with a mop protruding from the murky depths.

"That's awful!" she exclaimed, truly horrified.

The next morning the bucket was still there.

"That's disgusting," she muttered. "This is Zen?"

The next morning, the same bucket.

"I can't believe this! This is ridiculous. Someone should do something about this."

The fourth morning, there was the bucket, hardly improved by the days of neglect. The woman looked at the bucket and thought, "I'm someone," and took it away and cleaned it.

People 40, 50, 60 years old
are waiting for their parents
to parent them.

" I don't want to have to love
myself . I want my mother to
love me. I want my father
to give me what I need. "

The odds are very good
that that's not going to happen.

If your parents could love you
the way you want to be loved:

it would already have happened.

Only you
know how you want
and need to be loved.

Only you
can love you the way
you want and need
to be loved.

If you can't, if you won't (overcome
your conditioning in order to) give
yourself what you need, how do
you suppose <u>someone else</u> —

who isn't nearly so motivated,
who, in fact, is looking to get it for
themselves (possibly from you!) —

is going to provide it for you?

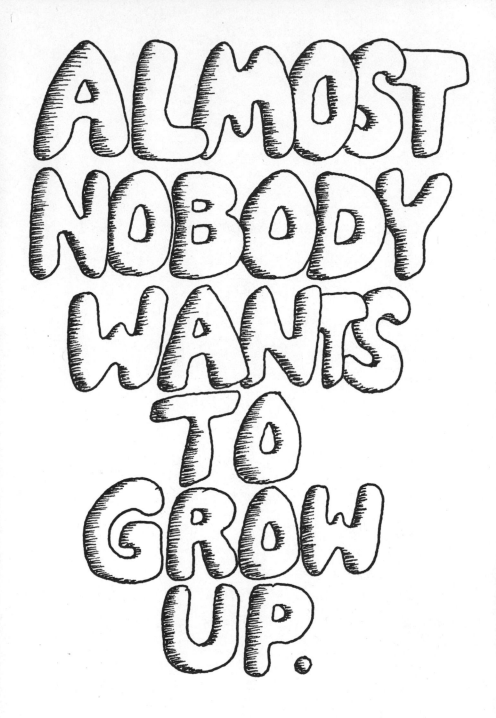

Living from compassion for ourselves
gives us each
the loving parent
we've always wanted.

I used to think I was going to find
within myself
a grownup to parent my child.

I've discovered that it's really a case of
finding the child
who can care for the grownup!

The secret is this.
The adult is the
abused product of society's conditioning,
while
the child, who was (thank goodness)
abandoned so that this person could
survive, is still here inside, whole and
complete and original.

You have to take
responsibility
for living
TODAY
the life you want to live.

WHAT I WANT IN MY LIFE	CHECK(✓) ONE		
	YES	NO	MAYBE
ACCEPTANCE			
REJECTION			
COMPASSION			
JUDGMENT			
CLARITY			
SHOULDS			
FREEDOM			
RESISTANCE			
MASTERY			
OTHER			

The only difference between
the life you are living
and
the life you want to live
is the feeling of being
appreciated, loved and accepted.
unconditionally.

So...

give it to yourself
             RIGHT NOW!
             THIS MINUTE!
             DON'T WAIT!

Not when you've changed.
Not when you're in a better mood.
Not when you've earned it.

                    RIGHT NOW!

You could start with appreciating yourself
      for reading this book,
      for caring,
      for being willing,
      for opening your heart.

There is nothing in life
that could happen to you
that is worse than living
in fear and self-hate.

And the great sadness is
that living in fear and self-hate
won't keep what you fear and hate
from happening to you.

We cling to our belief
that there is something wrong

There is something
wrong with this
universe, and
I need to fix it.

because that's how
we maintain our position
at the center of the universe.

Suffering provides our identity.
Identity is maintained
in struggle,
in dissatisfaction,
in trying to fix what's wrong.

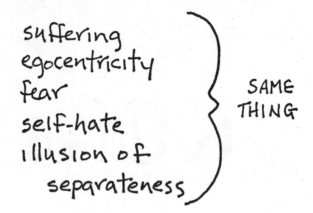

suffering
egocentricity
fear
self-hate
illusion of
   separateness

} SAME
  THING

So we are constantly looking for
what is wrong, constantly
creating new crises so we can rise
to the occasion.

                    To ego,
                    that's survival.

It is very important
that something be wrong
so we can continue to survive it.

I suspect we focus on
"learning from our mistakes"
(beating ourselves up over them)

because that keeps us
from paying attention to what
we are doing

NOW.

Remember,

as long as you are
out of the moment,
egocentricity
is in control.

GUIDE: Beating myself up over something is a really good scam because while I'm focused over here beating myself up, I'm really over here working at improving my character, and conveniently not noticing that over here... So, it works in two ways.

STUDENT: It's so hard to notice, until you've had it pointed out to you several million times, that this way of improving your character which you've been taught to do since childhood and have been diligently doing all you life, doesn't have the desired effect. You have to keep doing it all the time.

GUIDE: In fact, it has the opposite effect, which is why we do it. It's hard for people like us to feel like victims. We have to really search our experience, but if I don't feel like a victim, how do I justify my privileged position in life? I couldn't, and so I victimize myself constantly. I work so hard and I try so hard and I just punish myself constantly and, my god, I need a trip to Nepal to try to get some meaning in this life, you know. Or I need a new car because I have this hideous commute.

STUDENT: We have learned so deeply that if you don't punish yourself, you're not a good person, that those two things are equal. The more you hate yourself for doing bad stuff, the better, more virtuous person you are.

GUIDE: Of course, as soon as we take a look at it, we realize it never worked and it still doesn't work and, in fact, we have no evidence that it ever worked on anybody. It didn't work on us when we were kids, and it hasn't worked on us since we've been adults. It doesn't work on any kids we know. It doesn't work. Why do we continue to do it then?

STUDENT: Because it does work in a superficial way. You can beat yourself up for doing something bad and scare yourself enough so that you won't do that bad thing again. So on this level, you can say that it does work.

GUIDE: I think it does work, but not in the way we like to pretend it does. It works in that it enables me to do anything I want to do because I have to make up to myself for all the punishment I've received in life. It goes like this: I punish myself in ways that reinforce my identity, then I indulge myself in ways that maintain my identity. It is a constant balancing act in which I will be hard on myself in these ways, and I will indulge myself in these ways.

Most of us are pretty good at balancing these two. The result: maintenance of egocentricity.

≈ ♥ ≈

When you are in the present moment,
there is no you that is separate
                        and alone,
no identification with egocentricity.

        Self-hate is designed
    to make sure that doesn't happen.

Self-hate will pull you out of the
experience of the present moment in
order to get you to focus on
        "What's wrong? What did I do?"

It's that self-conscious questioning and
analysis that brings you out of the
present moment
either into the past,
        "How should I have been
            instead of how I was?"
or into the future,
        "What should I do about it?"

It doesn't matter what
did or did not happen then.

It only matters
what happens

NOW.

The best reason to look at self-hate is that it gets in the way of being able to do spiritual practice.

It gets in the way of finding that place of deep compassion within ourselves that is the largest part of spiritual practice.

When I first came to a spiritual practice, I thought I would learn to sit and all my conditioning, my suffering, my past would just go away and I would simply be centered.

Now I see that sitting means sitting <u>with</u> all of that, allowing it to be exactly as it is, not needing to do something about any of it.

Every time I try to fix myself, I compound the problem.

When the conditioning can just come up and pass away, it loses power, it loses momentum.

In this way, sitting still with it dissolves it, burns it away, strips it away.

This is why meditation
            paying attention
            awareness
                        is the answer,
this is why long retreats are helpful:

You sit still.
You are watching, watching, watching.
After several days the world sort of
goes away.
The system cannot maintain the same
connections because it tends to start
focusing on whatever is going on
around you, and there's not much
going on.
So everything starts slowing down,
everything starts
simplifying.
There's really
nothing to do
except turn
your attention
inward...

Then you begin to see what the programming is really like.
You begin to hear more clearly the things you tell yourself, things you couldn't hear until everything became
very quiet.

The watching creates
a spaciousness.

Your attention focuses.

It's like having a microscope:
now you can begin to see
what's really going on.

We have a choice.

We can live our lives trying to conform
to some nebulous standard
or
we can live our lives seeing how
everything works.

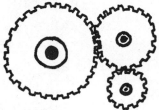

When we step back and look at it that
way, it is obvious that

the attitude of fascination
is the only intelligent one to bring
to anything.

STUDENT: When I first started sitting I figured out how many breaths it would take until I had to get up again.

GUIDE: A useful pursuit.

STUDENT: I would breathe one hundred and whatever breaths. Then I was able to let go of that and I started counting to 10. And then I realized that this had become a crutch. I figured out how many sets of ten it would take, and when I couldn't stand it anymore I thought, "I'll just breathe 5 more sets of ten and that will get me through this." But I realized that this was not helpful, and I was judging myself saying, "You're doing this wrong," and making a rule that I couldn't count to ten. I decided I should just count from 1 to 2.

And then I thought, "If the choice is not to sit or counting from 1 to 10, I'm going to count from 1 to 10."

GUIDE: Counting from 1 to 10 is not going to make me enlightened, but not counting from 1 to 10 is not going to make me enlightened either.

STUDENT: Ego says, "This is so stupid. This is a waste of time." And yet my experience is not that at all.

GUIDE: Exactly. If ego were to say, "I don't want to meditate anymore, I'm terrified, I'm afraid I'm going to die," it would be clear to us. But instead it says, "This is stupid. How long have I been doing this? Sitting here counting 1,2,3,4,..."

And it's very convincing. So then to be able to come back to center enough to say, "If somebody in me thinks this is boring and stupid, but somebody else in me wants to do it, why not let her?" So, to learn how to sit still when we hate what's going on, to learn to sit still when it's really, really hard is very good. There's nothing to do but let go of every idea you hold on to that you have any control. Breathe in, breathe out, breathe in, breathe out. Are you going to feel better? No. Are you going to get everything that you want? No. The good news is, there's no alternative. So you can say, "Okay, I'll just be all right with this," giving up all hope, all expectation, all illusion that you can affect anything. Breathe in. Breathe out. It's not a bad deal. So learning to sit still when there is nothing that you can do about what you're experiencing is incredibly valuable.

Ego will say, "Sitting used to be fun. I used to love to sit. It was easy to sit. I wanted to sit. I would go to retreats so I could sit a lot. Now I hate it. I don't want to be having this experience of sitting. I want to feel like I felt before." But you don't. Can you learn, in whatever way, without it turning into perversity, to love the experience that you're having? To open yourself completely to the experience of hating what's going on? To just let go completely into that experience and find out what that's like? Can you get a feel for it? Let yourself hate it. Let yourself be angry. Let yourself have a fit.

It would be good for you. It would be very therapeutic for you.

STUDENT: What I saw as you were talking is that I have this idea of how sitting is supposed to be.

GUIDE: Exactly, but how sitting is, is how sitting is. And how it is for you right now is miserable. So you get to experience feeling miserable. And if all you're being is miserable, miserable is not bad. It's only when you're miserable and hating miserable that it's really hell.

There's nothing more important than compassion. Anything other than compassion is designed to pull us off center. Everything other than compassion is ego. Don't fall for it. You can embrace it all in compassion, just like you would a mischievous child. But, if there is judgment, it is coming from ego. From center, from compassion, there is no judgment. There is no element of wrong or bad. So you don't have to be fooled any longer. Ego will be the one who's saying, "Well, yeah, but that isn't a *judgment.* That's just clarity of perception. I'm actually centered and I can see that from a centered place, it's really not good to be that way." WRONG.

STUDENT: It seems very helpful to have an external person saying, "Do you see how you're looking from ego here?" Is the idea to eventually have that kind of perspective internally?

GUIDE: Absolutely. What you're learning to do through this practice is see the place from which the guide looks. When you're with the guide you can see that very clearly. You move in and out of that place. Right? And you're finding that place inside of you. And eventually that will become your— and this has to be in quotes— "identity." You will simply live from that place. You will be pulled off occasionally into ego, but you will live from there.

≈ ♥ ≈

When you simply watch
the next movement
of the mind,

the whole mass of conditioning
you've been taught to believe
begins
            to   fall
                      away...

It is a miracle:

- to want to sit in meditation

- to sit in meditation and have your
  attention wander and then come
  back to the breath

- to get your head above water
  (or out of the
  stew pot) for
  any length
  of time.

- to have even a glimmering of how
  it all works

- to have the willingness to practice
  at all...

Jesus said,

"You must become as little children."

He was talking about having as our
primary identity the innocent
Heart, not the conditioned mind.

From the innocent, compassionate
Heart it is clear that life just
happens.
We don't need to take it personally.
We are not being punished, AND
we are not being rewarded.
                    And, yes,
          everyone gets old and sick
          and dies. But it is only
when we are identified with our
socialized, conditioned minds that
we have difficulty with any of it.

STUDENT: I've been thinking about the line from St. John, "Perfect love casts out fear." To me that means going back to the breath at any moment because there is the perfect compassion that will cast out fear. How else can we challenge that subtle kind of fear?

GUIDE: Going back to the breath means letting go beliefs, and without beliefs, you cannot be afraid.

STUDENT: It's really hard to put love in the place of fear, but just going back to the breath isn't hard at all— there's nothing to do but breathe.

GUIDE: Exactly. Trying to make love be there is doing something. Dropping everything and coming back to the breath is not doing anything. But in that place is the unconditional love you are seeking.

STUDENT: So if we want to have any kind of life that is moving toward freedom, we have to be continually returning to the breath.

GUIDE: Yes. That is the direction of finding compassion. It's important to see that compassion is not something we do. In fact, when you drop everything and come back to the breath, there's nothing going on, is there? Afterwards, we can say that it was peaceful or joyful or it felt like unconditional love, but when we're just with the breath, nothing is there. We want to make it something so we can have a subject-object relationship with it. But in the experience there is literally nothing going on. There's no self-hate, no problem in the future, no problem in the past. And we can accustom ourselves to being in that place; it becomes more and more familiar, and there is a sense of deeper identity— the identity that all beings share.

We practice coming back to that place again and again and again. And every time, everything falls away. Then we wander away off into all this stuff again, then we drop it and come back to the breath. We practice doing that with little things so we can experience that it's all right. So, I'm thinking about something, and I realize I'm just thinking so I drop the thought and come back to my breath. And nothing is lost. I'm not repressing anything. I'm not avoiding anything. I'm simply dropping that identity maintenance system for egocentricity, and I'm coming back to the moment. As I learn that there's no danger in this process, no fear, no loss, I can practice it with bigger things until one day, in the middle of something big and scary, I can drop it and come back to the breath. The process is exactly the same as for little things. I no longer believe that because it's a bigger whatever, it's more true. I know the answer is to drop it and come back to the breath.

Egocentricity's job is to counter that by insisting that if you drop it and go back to the breath, you will die. That's why I have to practice dropping every different thing that comes up a million times. I practice and practice and practice, and when that voice comes up saying I'm going to die if I don't do such and such my response is, "I haven't died yet.

How many times have you told me I was going to die and I haven't? Your credibility is slipping."

STUDENT: It took me a long time to see that "I'm going to die" is not necessarily a verbal message. For me, it's more a physical sensation, and also emotional upheaval, which I had to see time after time to realize that the underlying message was that I would die.

GUIDE: "I can't stand it" is another form it can take.

STUDENT: And still that space between the "I" dropping it and going back to the breath involves an incredible leap of faith.

≈ ♥ ≈

Doing this work alone is difficult, but certainly not impossible. If you have a friend or therapist or counselor who understands this work, that person can assist you in keeping a perspective of disidentification that self-hate will be diligently attempting to remove from you. Remember that maintaining itself is the primary focus of self-hate. It is clever, slippery and tricky. In the beginning it will fool you more often than not. And that is okay. It's not a contest. What you're learning in this work is to have compassion for yourself no matter what.

Keeping that firmly in the front of your awareness, here are some suggestions to get you started:

♦ Ask yourself what are the things you've always wanted someone to say to you, but no one ever has.

♦ Ask the child inside you what it needs to hear you say to it.

♦ Make a tape. Tell yourself the things you've always wanted someone else to say. Include everything the child needs to hear to feel loved and appreciated.

♦ Listen to the tape every day. Add to it when you think of something else you want to hear.

♦ Write love letters to yourself.

♦ Think of at least one loving thing to do for yourself each day.

♦ Make a list of things you'd like to have and begin providing them for yourself.

♦ Each time you give a gift to someone else, give something (even if it's just little) to yourself.

♦ Stop and appreciate yourself for every thought and act of kindness.

♦ Say thank you to yourself when you do something kind.

♦ Each time you receive a gift, give something (even if it's just something little!) to someone else, and really let yourself feel the joy of doing it.

♦ Get comfortable saying, "I love you" to yourself and say it many times each day.

♦ Take out pictures of yourself when you were little, frame them, place them in prominent places, and let yourself begin to appreciate that little person.

♦ Journal regularly, especially noting the self-hating ways you speak to yourself and treat yourself, and each time you become aware of a new way, remind yourself that even though you were taught to treat yourself that way, you are now committed to treating yourself with unconditional love and acceptance.

♦ And, of course, we would encourage a time of quiet and solitude each day (preferably a time of meditation) in order to be more present to yourself.

≈ ♥ ≈

_____The only way out
_____ of this life of suffering
_____ is through the doorway of compassion.

And here's the trick:

    Some of us know that we must
    find the compassion in order
    to be free, but HOW!?

"Sure, I can see that I'm growing,
opening up, but I'm not there. In fact,
I usually can't find the compassion
when I need it most."

            That's true.
You can't <u>find</u> it because you <u>are</u> it.

The moment there is
nothing left of you
but compassion,
you ARE the doorway.
The door is wide open and you are free.

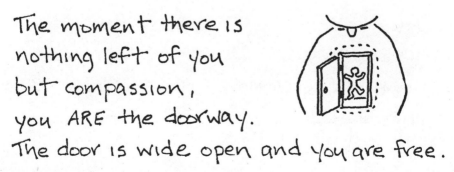

233

Reading about going beyond self-hate is like reading about swimming. You might get the general idea, but for the finer points, you're going to have to jump into the water.

InnerVision offers workshops on going beyond self-hate in a variety of formats. We also offer workshops and retreats on other topics including projection; belief systems; subpersonalities; the inner child; depression; attention and awareness; and meditation practice.

If you would like additional information on pursuing this work, please contact one of the following:

InnerVision
P.O. Box 91
Mountain View, CA 94042
(415) 966·1057

InnerVision
9400 Hwy. 19 W.
Bryson City, NC 28713